40 Days

A Daily Devotion for Spiritual Renewal

Troy Schmidt

Do not conform any longer to the pattern of this world, but be transformed by the renewing of your mind. Then you will be able to test and approve what God's will is— his good, pleasing and perfect will.
Romans 12:2

40 DAYS
A Daily Devotion for Spiritual Renewal

Copyright @ 2012 by Troy Schmidt
All rights reserved
Second edition
Printed August, 2012

Printed in the United States of America

Cover design / typesetting by Troy Schmidt

For more information about the Author, go to
www.troyeschmidt.com

Scripture taken from the HOLY BIBLE, NEW INTERNATIONAL VERSION®. Copyright © 1973, 1978, 1984 International Bible Society. Used by permission of Zondervan. All rights reserved.

ISBN-13: 9781478373445
ISBN-10: 147837344X

40 DAYS

CHAPTERS

Day 1..................................Renewal

40 DAYS WITH NOAH

Day 2..................................Righteousness
Day 3..................................Instruction
Day 4..................................Preparation
Day 5..................................Family
Day 6..................................Cleansing
Day 7..................................Salvation
Day 8..................................Trust

40 DAYS WITH MOSES

Day 9..................................Waiting
Day 10................................Time with God
Day 11................................Law
Day 12................................gods
Day 13................................Idols
Day 14................................God's Name
Day 15................................Sabbath
Day 16................................Parents
Day 17................................Murder
Day 18................................Sex
Day 19................................Stealing
Day 20................................Mouth
Day 21................................Coveting
Day 22................................Remembering
Day 23................................Responsibility
Day 24................................Fasting
Day 25................................Intercession
Day 26................................Again
Day 27................................Glow

40 DAYS WITH JOSHUA & CALEB

Day 28...............................Promises

40 DAYS WITH DAVID

Day 29...............................Story

40 DAYS WITH ELIJAH

Day 30...............................Future

40 DAYS WITH EZEKIEL

Day 31...............................Sin

40 DAYS WITH JONAH

Day 32...............................God's Word

40 DAYS WITH JESUS' TEMPTATION

Day 33...............................Deserts
Day 34...............................Bread
Day 35...............................View
Day 36...............................Promotion

40 DAYS WITH JESUS' RESURRECTION

Day 37...............................Seeing
Day 38...............................Kingdom
Day 39...............................Resurrection
Day 40...............................Go

Day 1

40 Days and You

Renewal

Do not conform any longer to the pattern of this world, but be transformed by the renewing of your mind. Then you will be able to test and approve what God's will is—his good, pleasing and perfect will.
Romans 12:2

A lot can happen in 40 days...
Focus on anything for 40 days—a diet, a workout, a book—and you can be pretty sure it will sink in. Unfortunately most of us give up before the benefits stick. We only give a diet a week to work, then after that we're back to the refrigerator. Then again, think how much changed in Germany in November 1989 with the fall of the Berlin Wall. In just days, communism collapsed.

40 days is a lot of time. Only the truly committed last at anything for 40 days. *Survivor*, one of the longest running reality shows, makes its competitors stay on the island for 40 days. Anyone who lasts that long dining on rats and raw squid deserves a million dollars! If they asked the people to survive for 7 days, it would seem too easy.

40 days requires perseverance and focus, staying the course for a desired goal. It's more than a month, but far less than a year.

40 days has a divine quality to it and for good reason—it's a very important number in the Bible. During a time period of 40 days, some of the most pivotal changes occurred that altered the course of the world forever.

For 40 days, God flooded the earth and renewed mankind.

For 40 days, God spoke to Moses and gave him a renewed covenant.

For 40 days, the Israelite spies checked out their new home—the Promised Land.

For 40 days, a Philistine taunted the Israelites and a new king emerged.

For 40 days, a prophet battled with depression then was renewed by a visit from God.

For 40 days, Jesus fasted in the desert and took on Satan, beginning a ministry that brought new life to the world.

And, for 40 days, the resurrected savior appeared to the masses, confirming his victory over death and giving the world a new hope for life after death.

This 40 day devotional focuses on a very specific goal—RENEWAL.

We like new things—a new car, a new house, a new job (with a new salary and new benefits). How about a new life? Many like the sound of a new life, but cringe at the requirements to achieve that. Why?

We grow comfortable in our old life. It's like sitting down in a nice new couch, settling in, taking a deep breath and relaxing. But after awhile—one year, two, maybe forty years later—you look down and what has happened? That new couch is old, tattered, ripped, with fleas battling for position. While everyone around us tells us to get off that couch and throw it out, we shrug and say, "Well, at least I'm comfortable."

A renewed life requires us to get up out of our old, flea-bitten ways in exchange for something new. So what's new about a renewed life? According to Romans 12:2, a transformation occurs with:

- A renewed mindset – a new way of seeing things
- A renewed hope – a new perspective on the future
- A renewed focus – a new view on God's will

It is a renewal that cannot come from the world. The pattern or tendency of the world cannot offer true, long-lasting spiritual answers to our deepest needs. You may feel new for a period, then it's back to the same ol', same ol'.

Whenever God took someone through 40 days, He changed them, giving them a renewed mindset, hope and focus. He spent 40 days with Noah, Moses, Elijah, David and Jesus, then used them to change the world.

Maybe God wants to spend 40 days with you to do the same.

So if you want to experience renewal, you must allow God to take hold of your old life and do something new with it. The renewal process outlined in this book begins with you accomplishing three daily tasks which may be new for you:

1. Pick up the Bible and READ the Scriptures at the end of every section. The word of God is living and active and pierces your mind and soul, important for you to change on the inside.
2. Finish the prayer prompt indicated at the end of every section and PRAY. Prayer encourages relationship with God, talking directly to him so you can receive guidance from the Holy Spirit.
3. DO the action challenge some time during the day. Action is the true sign of faith. Strengthen your faith by doing, not just believing.

Do you agree? Do you promise to go all the way? Don't give up and don't skip a day! If you are ready…then it's time to RENEW!

TODAY'S 40 DAY CHALLENGES

Read: **2 Corinthians 5:11-21**

Pray: **Dear God, I want a renewed life. My life feels old and stale. Please help me by…**

Do: **Find one old thing sitting around your house and throw it out. (Not your spouse.)**

Day 2

40 Days with Noah

Righteousness

The LORD saw how great man's wickedness on the earth had become, and that every inclination of the thoughts of his heart was only evil all the time. The LORD was grieved that he had made man on the earth, and his heart was filled with pain. So the LORD said, "I will wipe mankind, whom I have created, from the face of the earth—men and animals, and creatures that move along the ground, and birds of the air—for I am grieved that I have made them." But Noah found favor in the eyes of the LORD. This is the account of Noah.
Noah was a righteous man, blameless among the people of his time, and he walked with God. Genesis 6:5-9

Parents hurt when their kids rebel against them. It's hard to imagine the suffering a parent feels when their child turns to drugs or crime. The images flashing through their minds must include the child as a once innocent baby, cooing and laughing in their arms, so innocent...so harmless.
Now this.
It must have been hard for God to watch his creation deteriorate into debauchery and destruction. Killing, lying, cheating, sexual preoccupation had become the social norm for the earth. With no end in sight and no possible solution, God decided to start over.
Etch-O-Sketch has a wonderful "do-over" mechanism. Just shake the board and all the writing goes away. God decided to perform an Etch-O-Sketch on the world - shake things up and start over.

But instead of re-creating the entire earth, God whittled down the population to just one guy and his family. Noah.

All we know about Noah is this: Noah found favor in God's eyes. Noah was righteous and blameless. Now this can't mean that Noah was perfect, like Jesus perfect, but he believed God, sought God in daily matters and sacrificed to God. It didn't mean that Noah was better at acting righteous, putting on a morality show. Simply it meant that in God's eyes and on God's terms Noah had a right relationship with the Lord. Not one other person had that kind of relationship on the whole earth.

Things had gotten pretty desperate on earth and one man got God's attention.

God did not want to start something new until He found a righteous person to do the job. The 40 days of destruction started with God determining who would carry on the human population after the flood.

Today, God is still looking for those righteous people to take on tasks He has on His "to-do" list. The list of God's projects is very long. The list of those willing to take on those projects is quite short. We think pastors and seminary students and Billy Grahams get all the top jobs. Not the case. Noah wasn't a pastor or an evangelist. He was just a family guy.

God has something for you to do, but first He wants you to solidify your relationship with Him. Remember "righteous" is not a self-applied term (that would make it "self-righteous"). "Righteous" means that all debts are paid between two parties, there are no disagreements between them and the two are in a right relationship. It doesn't mean you're perfect! It means the one who is perfect has determined that you are *all-right* with him.

Some of you are thinking you can never be "righteous." You don't feel qualified for the Holy Person's Hall of Fame. God outlined the qualifications for righteousness with Abraham. Abraham heard God's promises and believed that God would fulfill those promises. Genesis 16 says that because of Abraham's faith, he received "righteousness."

The same holds true today. If we trust God, we respect him, love him and desire him. That's all God asks for. Are you righteous? To be in a right relationship with God, you must:

- Believe and trust God in all that He says
- Ask for forgiveness for all those times we trusted ourselves more than God
- Commit ourselves to God's plan and purpose

If you want to see new things happen in your life, it begins by renewing your relationship with the Lord and making it right. God will shake things up and give you a "do-over."

TODAY'S 40 DAY CHALLENGES

Read: **Romans 4:1-8**

Pray: **Dear God, I want to commit my life to you. That begins by confessing those times I trusted myself more than you, like...**

Do: **Make a "to-do" list of things you think God wants you to-do. Are you the right person for those jobs?**

Day 3

40 Days with Noah

Instructions

Now the earth was corrupt in God's sight and was full of violence. God saw how corrupt the earth had become, for all the people on earth had corrupted their ways. So God said to Noah, "I am going to put an end to all people, for the earth is filled with violence because of them. I am surely going to destroy both them and the earth. So make yourself an ark of cypress wood; make rooms in it and coat it with pitch inside and out. This is how you are to build it....Noah did everything just as God commanded him. Genesis 6:11-15, 22

When it comes to toys and their assembly, men can get very prideful. The challenge of the construction seems to dissuade the male species from using the instructions. "It's just a bike...how hard can it be" are usually the last uncensored words a man will say. Soon he discovers that there aren't supposed to be extra parts and bikes should stop when you apply the brakes.

In order to begin the 40 days of renewal that God wanted to bring to the earth, God came to Noah with a list of instructions. In this section of Genesis 6, God asked Noah to make an ark:

- Out of cypress wood
- With rooms
- Covered with pitch (or tar)
- 450 feet long, 75 feet wide and 45 feet high
- With a roof
- A door on the side
- Three decks

- Filled with two of every kind of animal

Imagine if Noah decided to improvise and use his expertise at boat building (there's no indication that he was a ship maker). Maybe four decks instead of three or skip the roof or cut back on the length and save some money and time. Or why not three of every animal, just to play it safe. That sort of thinking could have disrupted the fate of the world. What if the top-heavy boat capsized? Or the imbalance of creatures caused an animal riot? Or the cost-saving tar sprung leaks? The instructions were very specific and needed to be followed or the plan would not work.

If we want to experience a renewal in our lives, we must follow the instructions very closely...no improvisation, no cost cutting, no time saving.

David did not follow the instructions and sinned with Bathsheba. God sent the prophet Nathan to him with a story that convicted David to the core of his soul. David realized he was far from God and he wanted to reestablish their relationship. It was then that David wanted renewal. Psalm 51 includes very specific instructions on how David pleaded for that renewal.

- Ask God for mercy
- Confess your sins against God
- Ask for a pure heart
- Ask for joy in your life
- Ask what you can do sacrificially for God

Never think that renewal comes accidentally or coincidentally. Renewal begins after God invites you into the renewal process with very specific instructions and you accept that invitation by following those instructions very specifically.

If you don't, your ship could sink and those onboard may mutiny.

TODAY'S 40 DAY CHALLENGES

Read: Psalm 51

Pray: Dear God, I ask for your mercy. Forgive me for not following your instructions for my life. I have…

Do: Tell someone you're sorry for what you did to them recently or in the past.

Day 4

40 Days with Noah

Preparation

In the six hundredth year of Noah's life, on the seventeenth day of the second month—on that day all the springs of the great deep burst forth, and the floodgates of the heavens were opened. And rain fell on the earth forty days and forty nights...For forty days the flood kept coming on the earth, and as the waters increased they lifted the ark high above the earth. The waters rose and increased greatly on the earth, and the ark floated on the surface of the water. They rose greatly on the earth, and all the high mountains under the entire heavens were covered. The waters rose and covered the mountains to a depth of more than twenty feet. Genesis 7:11-12, 17-20

  Anyone who lived in Florida during 2004 knows something about hurricanes. During that unparalleled year, four major hurricanes tore into Florida (Charley, Frances, Ivan, Jeanne). For nearly 40 days, Floridians experienced the impact of ecological disasters. Just when one hurricane was gone, another seemed to be brewing in the Atlantic. Nervous homeowners and insurance agents prepared and settled in for one windy attack after another.
  It never seemed to end. Hurricane Frances' clouds covered the entire state, strengthening to a Category 4 that lasted all day and all night for nearly three days. Floridians could not sleep, worried that a tree may crash, any second, through their roof. Power was out for days. Generators roared through neighborhoods. No one showered in order to preserve the water.

That experience in 2004 gave us a glimpse of what Noah went through for 40 days. The constant pounding sound of rain...the damage occurring outside...being stuck inside with smelly, un-showered beasts...

Imagine what it would have been like to be confined inside a floating box, with thousands of stinky animals, while the entire world was being destroyed. Feelings of isolation and loneliness come to mind, as well as scared and worried. Even though Noah was told the length of this event, it could not prepare him for the day-by-day fear and incredible monotony that hung over his life.

We face storms too. Those storms come in the form of a relationship tornado or an economic earthquake or a medical tsunami. They hit hard and hit broadly across our lives. And as the storms are pounding down, we wonder...what will happen and will they ever end?

Thankfully God prepared Noah for the storm. Noah made sure he had all the necessary supplies onboard before the storm hit.

The time to prepare for a storm is never during the storm. You can't find plywood at Home Depot the day the hurricane hits and Noah could not build the ark while raindrops fell on his head. When the storm surged, Noah was ready.

We have to be ready for our storms now. We prepare for those storms by reminding ourselves of God's promises. Storms do not blow those promises away. They are simply testing grounds for the truth of those promises, in the same way a sickness tests the love and commitment of a married couple who promised to love each other in sickness and health on their wedding day. So what are those promises that prepare us?

The book of Deuteronomy includes Moses' last words to his people before he died, in order to prepare them for the battles ahead in the Promised Land. The book uses the word "remember" many times, telling the people to:

- Remember the time God has helped you
- Remember God's forgiveness when you fell
- Remember those from the Bible who God loved
- Remember the commandments
- Remember the battles God fought for you
- Remember the promises for the future

Since remembering is the solution, forgetting must be the problem. You must prepare yourself for the future storm by inventorying all that God has done for you—those times he helped you, forgave you, protected you and strengthened you in the past.

Every reassurance puts another plank on our faith, applies more pitch and tar to the trouble areas and strengthens the roof over our lives.

TODAY'S 40 DAY CHALLENGES

Read: Matthew 6:25-34

Pray: Dear God, thank you for always being faithful. I remember the times that you…

Do: Write down five times in the past when God was there for you.

Day 5

40 Days with Noah

Family

On that very day Noah and his sons, Shem, Ham and Japheth, together with his wife and the wives of his three sons, entered the ark. They had with them every wild animal according to its kind, all livestock according to their kinds, every creature that moves along the ground according to its kind and every bird according to its kind, everything with wings. Pairs of all creatures that have the breath of life in them came to Noah and entered the ark. The animals going in were male and female of every living thing, as God had commanded Noah. Then the LORD shut him in. Genesis 7:13-16

When it comes to Noah's story, we sometimes forget that he was not the only human onboard the ark. Noah's family joined him. Just as the animals were gathered in twos, for biological reasons of repopulation, so were Noah, Shem, Ham and Japheth and their wives. From those three sons would emerge a new humanity.

It does not say that the righteousness of Noah's family was the reason they were chosen to be spared from the flood. Only Noah's righteousness is mentioned.

The repercussions of one's faithfulness to God create an umbrella of blessing that extends beyond oneself to those around him or her. Noah's family was spared because Noah followed God in all that he did.

Your faithfulness and standing before God affect those around you too, from your spouse, to your children, to your in-laws, to your grandchildren, and, yes, even to the family pets. Everyone around a blessed person gets blessed too.

As we look at the reasons why we want renewal in our lives, we should look beyond ourselves. Renewing our lives protects those around us.

Many times when we sense a relational disconnect or family dissension, we pray that the other person would change instead of asking how we can change. We must look to ourselves as an epicenter of renewal, causing ripple effects into the lives of those living around us.

We see this in the New Testament, especially in Acts.

One of those listening was a woman named Lydia, a dealer in purple cloth from the city of Thyatira, who was a worshiper of God. The Lord opened her heart to respond to Paul's message. When she and the members of her household were baptized, she invited us to her home... Acts 16:14-15a

At that hour of the night the jailer took them and washed their wounds; then immediately he and all his family were baptized. The jailer brought them into his house and set a meal before them; he was filled with joy because he had come to believe in God—he and his whole family. Acts 16:33-34

Then Paul left the synagogue and went next door to the house of Titius Justus, a worshiper of God. Crispus, the synagogue ruler, and his entire household believed in the Lord; and many of the Corinthians who heard him believed and were baptized. Acts 18:7-8

It started with one family member saying yes to Christ to begin the process of seeing a whole family come to salvation.

Joshua, Moses' successor, saw a lot of idol worship going on around him. He stood before the tribes and, in his final moments, told them to decide who they were going to follow—God or idols? The people had compromised and were sending Israel into a tailspin.

Joshua stood unmoved by the current religious trends around him and said to everyone in Joshua 24: "Make up your minds as to who you are going to serve, but as for me and my house, we will serve the Lord."

Joshua took a stand for his family. The tribes saw his commitment and committed likewise. After that moment, they renewed their covenant with Lord.

Seek renewal not only for yourself, but for those around you.

It's a family affair.

TODAY'S 40 DAY CHALLENGES

Read: **Joshua 24**

Pray: **Dear God, I want renewal in my life and I want renewal in the lives of those around me, especially…**

Do: **Pray with a family member about whatever they want to pray about.**

Day 6

40 Days with Noah

Cleansing

For forty days the flood kept coming on the earth, and as the waters increased they lifted the ark high above the earth. The waters rose and increased greatly on the earth, and the ark floated on the surface of the water. They rose greatly on the earth, and all the high mountains under the entire heavens were covered. The waters rose and covered the mountains to a depth of more than twenty feet. Every living thing that moved on the earth perished—birds, livestock, wild animals, all the creatures that swarm over the earth, and all mankind. Everything on dry land that had the breath of life in its nostrils died. Every living thing on the face of the earth was wiped out; men and animals and the creatures that move along the ground and the birds of the air were wiped from the earth. Only Noah was left, and those with him in the ark. Genesis 7:17-23

There are two ways of looking at this great catastrophe.

One, it was the greatest disaster to ever hit the earth, killing 99.9999% of the human and animal population. Or two, it was the world's greatest bath.

Calamity or cleansing?

From a human perspective, we find it hard to believe that God wanted to wipe out every living thing from the earth. It appears inhumane, unjust and treacherous.

However, from a Godly perspective, we can see God's hatred of sin displayed in the flood.

If a surgeon has to remove a cancerous lung, the patient doesn't scream at the doctor, "You hate lungs, you evil lung-hater!" No, the surgeon doesn't want the cancer to spread to the rest of the body and, by removing the lung, he saves the patient. The act of removing the lung, cleanses the patient of cancer. It shows his love for the patient.

God wants the cancerous effects of sin to be removed from our lives before it spreads to all aspects of our body.

The December 2005 tsunami in Asia showed the devastating effects of rushing water in a community. Everything in its path is wiped out. Water is powerful.

We use water to clean because it is so effective against dirt. Everything from dishes to baths to a pressure washer breaks down dirt and cleanses it.

God wants that cleansing to occur in our lives. Not the dirt on the outside of our bodies, but the dirt on the inside. Our sin. Like the flood, He wants all sin to be washed away from us. Not just cleaned, but drowned and destroyed.

Baptism represents that cleansing. A person stands before others, sometimes in a white robe to help exemplify purity, then basically takes a quick bath. That baptism symbolizes what happened when a person accepted God's forgiveness through the sin-cleansing sacrifice of Jesus Christ on the cross.

During the flood, so much death had to happen before cleansing could occur. The animal sacrifices in the Old Testament all the way to the ultimate sacrifice of Jesus on the cross in the New Testament were bloody, deadly scenes. But from those bloodbaths came cleansing, since God determined that something must die as a penalty for sin (Leviticus 5). The penalty of sin is death. Once something dies, something new occurs. Death first...cleansing second.

The flood Noah saw was a destructive scene, but one of cleansing leading to renewal. It is what God wants for us today. A spiritual cleansing requires some steps:

- Confess your wrong and admit your responsibility
- Stop doing that wrong again

- Cut out certain aspects of your life that lead to that wrong

1 John 1:9 seems too easy to be true. It says if we confess, we will be forgiven and cleansed. That means in God's eyes, the stain of sin has been washed away. We are as clean and as white as snow.

But in truth those steps are hard because of our selfish, prideful nature. Even here a death must occur—a death of self. The old *you* dies and the new *you* emerges.

So surrender to God and jump into His bathtub of forgiveness. In the end, you'll be as good as new.

TODAY'S 40 DAY CHALLENGES

Read: 1 John 1

Pray: Dear God, I want a cleansing to occur in my life. That begins with confession. I confess that I…

Do: Write down your sins on a piece of a paper, admit them, and then throw them away.

Day 7

40 Days with Noah

Trust

But God remembered Noah and all the wild animals and the livestock that were with him in the ark, and he sent a wind over the earth, and the waters receded. Now the springs of the deep and the floodgates of the heavens had been closed, and the rain had stopped falling from the sky. The water receded steadily from the earth. At the end of the hundred and fifty days the water had gone down, and on the seventeenth day of the seventh month the ark came to rest on the mountains of Ararat. The waters continued to recede until the tenth month, and on the first day of the tenth month the tops of the mountains became visible. After forty days Noah opened the window he had made in the ark. Genesis 8:1-6

We tend to think Noah's ordeal was only a 40 day challenge, but it lasted much longer. The Bible says that water covered the earth for 150 days after the 40 days of rain and slowly started to seep into the earth or evaporate into the sky. The ark finally rested on the mountains of Ararat, Turkey. But it didn't end there.

40 days after resting on the mountain, Noah opened the window (whew, it must have stunk). Those 40 days must have seemed like the most unproductive days of Noah's 600 year old life. Can anything be more boring than waiting for water to evaporate?

What did Noah do for those 40 days? Let's remember, he's a righteous man so he probably did righteous man things.

- He prayed

- He hung out with his family
- He made sure the animals and the ark were okay
- He trusted

Trusting is a tremendously spiritual thing. *Doing* can sometimes be an unspiritual thing.
Trusting requires faith in God. *Doing* shows more faith in us and our actions.

What if Noah looked outside at all that sunshine and decided to let the animals out early? They would soon be dead and drowned animals.

Or what if Noah thought it was too nice a day to sit inside and decided to dismantle the ark to build a hut on that tiny patch of Mount Ararat? He would have a dead and drowned family on his hands.

Taking matters into his own hands, Noah could have devastated the earth forever. It was better for him to sit, wait and do nothing, in other words...trust.

God promised to take care of Noah and his family during the storm and that promise did not end once the storm ended. It continued into the period of waiting. During that time, the earth needed to heal and settle into its new state. There is nothing Noah could do to change that.

The faith Noah exhibited during those 40 days inside a closed ark, resting on a mountain, with an open window of opportunity, showed he trusted God when there seemed to be nothing going on. There was plenty going on, but it was out of Noah's hands. There was nothing Noah could do about it but wait.

Most people are waiting for something. A check. A report from their doctor. A letter from a college. Results from an interview. Test grades. A spouse. We want it now, but we can't have it now. We must wait and let God do what He needs to do.

During this time, God may need to change a mind or cause it to rain or rearrange a company's structure or get the right person to you, who currently lives 2,000 miles away and needs to transfer to your area.

If we try to move ahead of God, we can really mess things up.

Trust and let God work.

During that time pray, hang out with those you love and don't neglect those things you are responsible for currently as you trust for what's to come.

While you are waiting, you are renewing your trust for God. So just gaze out the window and pray for what's coming over the horizon.

TODAY'S 40 DAY CHALLENGES

Read: **Romans 8:18-28**

Pray: **Dear God, you know I what I am waiting for. I trust that you are…**

Do: **For five minutes, do nothing. Think about what God is doing right now in answer to your prayer.**

Day 8

40 Days with Noah

Salvation

...In it (Noah's ark) only a few people, eight in all, were saved through water, and this water symbolizes baptism that now saves you also—not the removal of dirt from the body but the pledge of a good conscience toward God. It saves you by the resurrection of Jesus Christ, who has gone into heaven and is at God's right hand—with angels, authorities and powers in submission to him. 1 Peter 3:20b-22

Life Savers, those little round candies with a hole in it, can't really save your life. Imagine if someone was drowning and the person pulled out a roll of Life Savers and tossed one in the water. No good.

Or if the person was struggling to breathe with an asthma attack... "Life Saver?" Or if the person was bleeding from a gun shot wound... "Peppermint or Cherry?"

The company should put a disclaimer on the side of the roll or they could be sued for false advertising. It should read, "Life Savers cannot actually save your life. In the case of an emergency, call 911."

Now if someone was drowning, a real life saver—a large, floatable ring—would come in very handy. The ring is built to float and sustain the weight of a person struggling to keep their head above water.

Noah's dual 40 day ordeals of waiting through the storm and waiting for the storm to recede brought about something very important in the end...life saving.

Noah knew nothing about making luxury liners, but he trusted God and, as a result, he floated above the destructive forces of the waters below him.

Noah knew nothing about zoo keeping, but he trusted God to provide and every animal was healthy when it stepped off.

Noah knew nothing about the future, but he trusted God and God safely kept him alive.

And without faith it is impossible to please God, because anyone who comes to him must believe that he exists and that he rewards those who earnestly seek him. By faith Noah, when warned about things not yet seen, in holy fear built an ark to save his family. By his faith he condemned the world and became heir of the righteousness that comes by faith. Hebrews 11:6-7

Did the ark keep Noah and his family alive? No, not really. It was his faith. Noah trusted God and he received salvation.

The cross and Noah's boat metaphorically do the same thing—save whoever clings to it.

Peter addressed a crowd in Acts 2.

"Therefore let all Israel be assured of this: God has made this Jesus, whom you crucified, both Lord and Christ. When the people heard this, they were cut to the heart and said to Peter and the other apostles, "Brothers, what shall we do?" Peter replied, "Repent and be baptized, every one of you, in the name of Jesus Christ for the forgiveness of your sins. And you will receive the gift of the Holy Spirit. The promise is for you and your children and for all who are far off— for all whom the Lord our God will call." Acts 2:36-39

Do you have faith in what Jesus did on the cross? The cross represents the eternal sacrifice for all of humanity's sins, bringing about forgiveness to all who believe.

Are you floating above the destructive waters of sin or are you drowning in them? What kind of life saver are you holding on to…one that can barely sustain your weight or Jesus who took on the weight of the world?

To receive the eternal life saver, you must realize you are drowning and in need of salvation. Only then will you grab on to the life saver Jesus has thrown over the side to rescue you.

But it's not a round floatation device.

It's shaped like a cross.

TODAY'S 40 DAY CHALLENGES

Read: John 14

Pray: **Dear God, I admit that I'm drowning in my sins. I trust that what Jesus did on the cross is the only way to save me. Thank you for…**

Do: **If this is the first time you have prayed to receive salvation, contact someone on a church staff or a trusted Christian friend and tell them about your new relationship with God.**

Day 9

40 Days with Moses

Waiting

When Moses went up on the mountain, the cloud covered it, and the glory of the LORD settled on Mount Sinai. For six days the cloud covered the mountain, and on the seventh day the LORD called to Moses from within the cloud. To the Israelites the glory of the LORD looked like a consuming fire on top of the mountain. Then Moses entered the cloud as he went on up the mountain. And he stayed on the mountain forty days and forty nights. Exodus 24:15-18

    One time I saw, in the country of Columbia, a group of people waiting outside a building. They were there all day. I ask my interpreter what they were doing. She said they were waiting to pay their utility bill. ALL DAY they waited.
    Can you imagine the outrage in the United States if a utility company made you wait all day? There would be lawsuits. Riots. Facebook rants!
    We value our time. We hate traffic jams, return lines at the store after Christmas, 15 item people in the 10 item Express Lane, waiters that move like molasses, mortgage approval delays, airport ticket counters. The worst thing anyone can say to you is: "Take a number."
    We hate to wait.
    Moses battled Pharaoh, led the Egyptians to a safe distance away into the wilderness and was ready to get things started with this new nation. He was in his 80s (40 years as the Pharaoh's adopted son and 40 years as a sheep herder). People in their 80s are REALLY impatient because their time is running out.

Then God called him into his office on top of a mountain and what did He do? Made him wait for six days.

"Take a number Moses, I'll be right with you."

Doctor's waiting rooms get to me. You book an appointment at 10:00, then at 10:30 they call you into the examination room, then at 11:00 the doctor shows up. What's with that? One time, after waiting an hour and a half, I left the doctor's office. They seemed shocked that I would do such a thing. "Our doctor's time is very valuable." "Yeah, so is mine!" I never returned.

However, if I did wait, I would be acknowledging how important the doctor was to me. If he was the best in the field and could promise me a cure for cancer, an hour and a half would seem like nothing. Heck, a day or two would be fine if it added more years to my life. If I were in the finest restaurant in Paris, a great meal would be worth the half hour delay, right? Even a little extra time at the grocery story is no problem if you're getting great food at a great price holding an incredible coupon.

One time at the Universal Studios theme park in Orlando, I waited 2 hours to get on the Spiderman ride, but it was the most amazing ride I have ever been on. I have long forgotten the length of the wait. I only remember the spectacle of the ride.

God made Moses wait…why?

Moses needed to get ready. A little quiet time relaxed his nerves. Maybe it gave him time to reflect and prepare his heart for an encounter with the magnificent, incredible, powerful God himself.

That's worth it. Right?

Maybe waiting helped Moses detach from the previous months' events and get a new perspective on where he had come from and where he was going. A little meditating.

Moses probably got a little sleep. He used the time for physical rejuvenation.

I don't think the wait was a big problem for Moses. (It will be for the Israelites as we'll see soon). God told Moses to "take a number" (the ticket read "1"), then Moses had to wait seven days to see the God of the Universe. Sounds worth it. I would wait.

We don't mind the wait if we're about to encounter something great.

So why do we freak out having to wait for God?

Maybe we have to get ready first.

Maybe we have to prepare ourselves for what God has to say.

Maybe we need a little rest or a new perspective.

Maybe we have to show God that He is worth the value of our time.

Are you waiting for renewal? Don't worry. God has not forgotten you.

So take a number and use waiting as a time of renewal. Don't worry. You're his number 1 priority.

TODAY'S 40 DAY CHALLENGES

Read: **Psalm 5**

Pray: **Dear God, you are worth the wait. Right now, you know I am waiting for...**

Do: **Next time you are waiting in line, pray for anything you are waiting on God to answer.**

Day 10

40 Days with Moses

Time with God

The LORD said to Moses, "Come up to me on the mountain and stay here, and I will give you the tablets of stone, with the law and commands I have written for their instruction." Exodus 24:12

Conferences for work are excellent opportunities to focus on your business, new changes in the future and thought paradigms. They allow you to interact with other people in your line of work, make new connections and show the boss how much you care.

But after a couple days, these conferences grow tiresome. Speech after speech. Information on top of information. Hotel breakfast buffet after hotel breakfast buffet.

Yikes.

Imagine what Moses went through dedicating himself to a 40 day personal conference with God on the mountaintop. At first, one would consider this a privilege, to be asked into God's presence to receive very specific information about the way God wants the world to live.

After a few days, it could grow tiresome, unless that time was more than just speech after speech by God, law after law, do this, don't do that, take notes. The information that God communicated to Moses during that time is found in Exodus chapters 19-31. It takes about thirty minutes to read (Leviticus expands that information more thoroughly), yet Moses must have done more for those 40 days than just taking thirty minutes of notes.

While we don't know for sure, here are some thoughts as to how Moses used his time with God:

- Resting – Moses had been through a lot and needed to relax. A little away time.
- Refreshing – Moses had been under attack and needed to be encouraged.
- Receiving – God told Moses the law. Moses took it all to heart. It's also possible that God gave him more details about what happened in the book of Genesis since Moses wasn't around for that.
- Questioning – Moses probably had some questions as to the specifics of the law and sought out those answers.
- Listening – Moses kept his mouth shut as God spoke.
- Thanking – Moses told God how thankful He was for being chosen and for saving the Israelites.
- Repenting – Moses felt sorry for his sins, especially for killing that guy.
- Counseling – Moses maybe felt grief for all the devastation he witnessed in Egypt. While he understood justice, seeing all those people perish and hearing the sounds of families grieving at Passover gets to a guy.
- Praising – Moses could not help praising God. The angels do it all the time in God's presence.
- Preparing – Moses was about to step into a new role of leadership—law giver. He needed to understand this new leadership model.

During your 40 days of renewal, what should you be doing? How should you spend your time with God?

- Resting – Physical rest is so important to spiritual clarity.
- Refreshing – Allow God's word to encourage you.
- Receiving – Understand God's word.

- Questioning – Ask questions and seek answers.
- Listening – Be quiet and let God speak.
- Thanking – Thank God for everything.
- Repenting – Confess your sins.
- Counseling – Let God's healing wash over you.
- Praising – Sing praises to God for who He is.
- Preparing – Get ready for what God wants you to do next.

If that's the case, don't look at these 40 days as a time of you just writing down a bunch of do's and don'ts for your life. Use these 40 days to address every physical and spiritual need of your body, mind and spirit.

You are one-fourth of the way through an amazing, life-changing conference with God!

TODAY'S 40 DAY CHALLENGES

Read: **Any Psalm you want.**

Pray: **Take ten minutes to just listen to God through that Psalm.**

Do: **While you listen, take out a pen and write down one thing you think God is saying to you. Take that paper with you all day and meditate on it.**

Day 11

40 Days with Moses

Law

The LORD gave me two stone tablets inscribed by the finger of God. On them were all the commandments the LORD proclaimed to you on the mountain out of the fire, on the day of the assembly. At the end of the forty days and forty nights, the LORD gave me the two stone tablets, the tablets of the covenant. Deuteronomy 9:10-11

    Taking notes is so important in school. The information you write down from the teacher's lectures can determine your understanding, your study habits, your test grades and your future in that line of work.
    Taking proper notes begins with carefully listening and thoroughly understanding everything said. If you leave something out, your grade will suffer. If you write down the wrong thing, you'll do the wrong thing.
    Imagine the pressure Moses was under to transcribe and transmit the law correctly. It required focus, precision and dedication to get it right.
    Here's an overview of the topics covered in the law that Moses received those 40 days from Exodus 20-31:

- The 10 commandments
- The construction of altars
- The rights of man in civil cases
- The rights of property and ownership
- Proper sexual conduct
- Proper business conduct
- Justice
- Sabbatical years

- Feasts of Unleavened Bread, Feasts of the Harvest, Feasts of the Ingathering
- Rules of war
- Offerings of the tabernacle
- The construction of the tabernacle (a temporary temple while they are without a city)
- The ark of the covenant
- The priests' garments
- The procedures of the priests
- Use of oils and incense in offerings
- Sabbath regulations

Why so much information? At first glance (and even more so when we read Numbers and Leviticus), all of these laws seem about as exciting as reading the local town building codes.

All of these rules show us that God cares about us. His rules protect us from harm and relational disputes. They keep us from hurting and being hurt.

They also show us that worshipping God is a serious matter. Every one of the items used in the tabernacle and on the priests' garments had meaning, and understanding that meaning led to a deeper appreciation for God.

We need to take careful notes, as Moses did, when it comes to the laws of God. Jesus simplified the commandments to two—love God and love your neighbors—so we tend to think if we go to church and wave to our neighbors as we drive by, we're covered. Jesus' simplifications pointed to complex behavioral patterns that needed to be exhibited day-by-day, 24/7. He made it easy for us to remember, but difficult in terms of perfecting.

Following the laws of God require us to change the way we relate to strangers, neighbors, family, the opposite sex, business partners, our pastors, church members, the guy in line ahead of you, the check-out girl, the homeless person.

Following the laws of God demand that we take church more seriously, the worship, the singing, the offering, the sermon, the small groups and those areas we serve in.

Don't glance over the laws of God too quickly. Renew your understanding of them and apply them to your life.

TODAY'S 40 DAY CHALLENGES

Read: Exodus 22

Pray: Dear God, I haven't been paying careful attention to your law. In fact I have been taking it too lightly, especially in the area of...

Do: Out of all the rules you read in Exodus 22, what's one thing that you can apply to your life today? Then do it.

Day 12

40 Days with Moses

gods

"You shall have no other gods before me. Exodus 20:3

  During his time on the mountain, Moses received what was the most important law book of all time. The Ten Commandments. These Ten Commandments simplified the complex rules of living a perfect God-ordained life. If we can renew our commitment and understanding of all ten of them, we can renew our lives.
  In the first commandment, God tells us not to have any other god before Him. Now "god" is a very general term. At the time, God probably wanted to disassociate himself from the Egyptian gods that the Israelites secretly respected or paid homage to in their worship. Certainly in their journey, the Israelites would meet new enemies or new neighbors with their new gods. Curiosity set in. Relationships occurred. And before you knew it, the Israelites were bowing at their temples.
  God says don't be tempted to worship anything other than Him. It's a problem the Israelites faced beginning with Moses and continued to the end of the Old Testament.
  When Jesus arrived, the Jews had overcome their temptation toward other gods. He spoke to a monotheistic crowd who followed the God of the Old Testament. However, Jesus knew their gods were different now.

"No servant can serve two masters. Either he will hate the one and love the other, or he will be devoted to the one and despise the other. You cannot serve both God and Money. The Pharisees, who loved money, heard all this and were sneering at Jesus. He said to them, "You are the ones who justify yourselves in the eyes of men, but God knows your hearts. What is highly valued among men is detestable in God's sight. Luke 16:13-15

Their gods had become money, greed and the pursuit of wealth. Their jobs as religious leaders provided riches. Money was their master.

Today there are things that "master" us, taking priority over God:

- Jobs, work
- Family, children
- Recreation (boats, vacations, second homes)
- Friends, boyfriends, girlfriends

WHAT! But these are all important things to our lives! True, however they cannot become more important than God.

"But I need to provide for my family…"

"But my children are very busy…"

"But it's so important to get away and have ME time…"

"But God wants me to have friends…"

Yes, yes, yes, yes. But, if we find that our time devoted to these things begins to take away from our time from God, then those things "master" us. In Matthew 6:33, Jesus tells His followers "But seek first his kingdom and his righteousness, and all these things will be given to you as well."

SEEK out what God wants you to do. Discover the way to become right (and stay right) in God's eyes. Pursue God's will for your life. Keep God the number one priority in your life.

THEN, as God promises at the end of Matthew 6:33, He will sustain and bless all those other things in your life— your job, your family, your time, your friends.

Look at your calendar and look at your checkbook to determine your god. Renew your devotion to one true God and remove those other gods from the throne of your life.

God is jealous not because His feelings of self-esteem are so fragile, but because He loves us so much. He hates to see us hurt and disappointed by our other masters.

TODAY'S 40 DAY CHALLENGES

Read: **2 Kings 17 and the consequences Israel faced worshipping other gods.**

Pray: **Dear God, I believe I have allowed other things to become more important than you. Forgive me for worshipping the gods of...**

Do: **Cancel something on your calendar that has become so important and give that time to God through worship or serving Him.**

Day 13

40 Days with Moses

Idols

"You shall not make for yourself an idol in the form of anything in heaven above or on the earth beneath or in the waters below. You shall not bow down to them or worship them; for I, the LORD your God, am a jealous God, punishing the children for the sin of the fathers to the third and fourth generation of those who hate me, but showing love to a thousand {generations} of those who love me and keep my commandments. Exodus 20:3-6

    The TV show "American Idol" has become a phenomenon. The world watches as underdogs and nobodies rise from obscurity and become pop stars. It's interesting to watch the person go from regular guy to superstar in a matter of months. Before, nobody paid attention to them as they went to the store. Now, everybody wants their autograph as they walk to the car.
    People cheer as they strut out on stage. Fans fall to the floor, dance on their feet, scream with joy, lift signs, and enjoy their presence. Later, the crowds show more adoration by buying their songs and going to their concerts.
    Sounds like Idol worship…
    At first glance, Commandment 1 and Commandment 2 appear very similar. Isn't this the same thing? Yes and no.
    Commandment 1 (no other gods before Him) is more of an internal heart priority while Commandment 2 is more an external practice. Both put God in second place.
    God describes an idol in Exodus 20:

- Something we make or create for ourselves. It's tangible and touchable. It's not spiritual. In the

Bible they were made of gold, silver, bronze, stone or wood.
- Something we literally bow down to out of adoration and devotion. In the Bible people made idols to Baal, Molech, Asherah, Rephan, Artemis or any of the Roman emperors.
- Something we worship, giving it our time and energy.
- Something we obey and do whatever it says. In the Bible, those idols instructed people to kill their own children and commit adultery.

Idols were and are objects that people worshipped by touching and feeling them. This is the practice of putting altars or statues of people in our home or cars and believing that those things keep us safe. It could be likened to certain rituals and superstitions like "knock on wood" or Friday the 13th. Other practices such as reading our horoscopes or going to a psychic or buying a self-help book that focuses on worldly principles could be considered idols. Maybe you have to consult one of those Magic 8 balls before you make a decision..."Signs point to yes."

They are the good luck charms we carry with us or put in our cars. How is a little statue on your dashboard going to stop an 18-wheeler with no brakes from turning you into a metal sandwich? It can't.

Remember, it's only an idol if we make it idol. If we feel it has power in our lives or we need it to survive or to have good fortune, then we've put too much confidence into it.

If we are going to renew our lives, we must throw out those old idols that divert our attention from God. Why?

This is what the LORD says:
"What fault did your fathers find in me,
that they strayed so far from me?

> They followed worthless idols
> and became worthless themselves. Jeremiah 2:5

Our spiritual lives become worthless as we follow worthless idols. Has something crept into your life that you follow and obey, to the point that you cannot make a move until you've consulted with this other thing?

God is a living God. He sees, He thinks, He cares, and He has the entire universe at His disposal. Why would we go anywhere else for direction? God asked the Israelites, after a victory over their enemy, to march through the country and destroy all the idols.

Maybe on your quest for renewal, you need to do the same.

TODAY'S 40 DAY CHALLENGES

Read: **Jeremiah 14:14-22.**

Pray: **Dear God, as I read this I realized that I put my trust in something other than you. That object, Lord, has become my idol…**

Do: **Throw out any idols in your house—Buddha, horoscope, Ouija board.**

Day 14

40 Days with Moses

God's Name

"You shall not misuse the name of the LORD your God, for the LORD will not hold anyone guiltless who misuses his name. Exodus 20:7

Don't you hate it when people get your name wrong? Even more uncomfortable is when they've been calling you the wrong name for a long time and you don't want to hurt their feelings and tell them your real name. Many times, when people don't quite get my name, they think it's Todd. Now Todd and Troy don't even rhyme. I could understand Goy, Joy, Boy, Roy or Leroy, but Todd? Whatever the reason, I quickly become Todd in their eyes, to the point that I sometimes surrender and admit, "Yes, I am Todd." I'll even answer to it.

Commandment number 3 has to do with using God's name properly. It's not about calling God the wrong name, but using His name in the wrong way.

It's clear that this verse tells us not to curse using God's name. The "GD" or "JC" terms used to get bleeped out of television all the time, because of the significance attached to this commandment. There's still a little secular reverence holding on these days, but slowly that term is slipping into the mainstream.

Some take this commandment to the other extreme and say that "Gosh" and "Golly-gee-willikers" and "Gee whiz" all defame God since they are euphemisms. I don't know about you, but "Gee Whiz" sounds nothing like "God" just like Todd sounds nothing like Troy.

Thousands of years ago, from the time of Jewish scholars to monks, the name of God was so holy, nobody felt worthy to even utter it. If one was transcribing the name of

God, they would stop and wash their hands, cleansing them of filth before writing the holy name of God. At least they were showing reverence, but maybe this, once again, goes too far.

The commandment doesn't say we can't use the Lord's name, we just can't misuse it. So how can we misuse it?

The point of the commandment is that if we use a term over and over, that after awhile it becomes cliché or mundane. If we use God's name as an exclamation, over and over, the name reduces its meaning from the title of the Creator, Redeemer and Father of the world to a mere exclamation before a sentence. "God, I can't believe it" or "Jesus, did you see that?" If you are not addressing God or Jesus, then those terms are unnecessary to the sentence. His name loses significance.

The other misuse of God's name is if we speak for God without telling the truth. "God says you must..." "God told me to..." "God is telling us..." "Or I swear to God..."

"Do not swear falsely by my name and so profane the name of your God. I am the LORD." Leviticus 19:12

Swearing here means make a promise. You can "swear to God" (it doesn't mean you can "swear at" God) but you had better do it honestly. You profane His name if you attach it to a lie. His name loses *truth*.

If His name is always attributed to a curse, as when we say God is damning people, then people begin to think that's all God does is send people to hell. His name loses *love*.

Profanity means to make something common or vulgar. In earlier times, it meant the language that you would hear in the streets or the bars. Today it means dirty talk. However, the root of the word "profane" means an unnecessary and useless term.

Jerry Seinfeld said that when he does comedy, he never uses profanity because he finds it's a cheap laugh. The heart of his comedy is in the story, situation and character, not in a handful of bad words. It's easy, he says, to curse and get a laugh, but people are not laughing at the comedy, but at the words.

We must adjust our talk so that our words are not profane. We must renew our tongues so that there are no useless words in our language.

God's name should never be reduced to common, everyday language, but be reserved for times of worship, adoration and prayer. If we pepper our language with "God" and "Jesus" all the time, then his name loses *power*.

Imagine how the Muslims would feel if Muhammad became an expression. "Muhammad this" and "Muhammad that." Why don't we scream "Buddha" when we stub our toe? Why not curse saying, "May Zeus send you to Hades!" That seems ridiculous, so why should we substitute God's name in those instances?

Remember, God's name has significance, truth, love and power. Renew your speech and use His name only to give Him the glory.

TODAY'S 40 DAY CHALLENGES

Read: **Exodus 3:1-15.**

Pray: **Dear God, may your name never lose its meaning. When I speak your name, I acknowledge your worthiness, your strength and your love for us...**

Do: **Over the next 40 days, examine your speech. How do you use the name of God, Jesus and Christ?**

Day 15

40 Days with Moses

Sabbath

"Remember the Sabbath day by keeping it holy. Six days you shall labor and do all your work, but the seventh day is a Sabbath to the LORD your God. On it you shall not do any work, neither you, nor your son or daughter, nor your manservant or maidservant, nor your animals, nor the alien within your gates. For in six days the LORD made the heavens and the earth, the sea, and all that is in them, but he rested on the seventh day. Therefore the LORD blessed the Sabbath day and made it holy." Exodus 20:8-11

    It's interesting to see how far some take this commandment. When I was in Israel, I visited during the Jewish celebration of Pentecost, which is a weeklong Sabbath. The orthodox Jews took the idea of Sabbath very seriously and did absolutely no work. They stayed in hotels so others could wait on them. They wouldn't tear toilet paper so toilet paper came pre-ripped. They did not push the buttons on the elevator, so the elevator opened and closed on every floor. They could walk to the elevator, but pushing the button was considered physical exertion. They refused to grind coffee because, well, why should the grinder be asked to exert itself?
    Jesus faced this similar thinking when He healed and performed miracles on the Sabbath. What's interesting is that the Pharisees never denied the miracles he performed—only the performance of a miracle on a day when no one should do any miracles. Doing miracles, they believed, required work, which is odd because a miracle means God is doing all the work. Maybe it's a sin to ask God (and the coffee pot) to do work?

Now the idea of taking a break from work sounds very pleasing. Sabbath and vacation go hand-in-hand. We have a hard time taking vacations. A friend of mine told me he was taking off the day before Christmas, but said he was going into work anyway for a little bit. Somehow, for him, working on his vacation didn't really seem like working. Huh?

God took a break after creating the earth for six days. Did God need a break? If God is spirit and without lungs and sweat glands, why did He need a breather? God rested on the seventh day as an example of what He wanted us to do, because He knew how hard it would be for us to do that.

The Sabbath has three main purposes. Even today we should try to honor these purposes as best we can.

The Sabbath is a day of *reflection*. There should be one day that we worship and reflect on the Lord. One day out of seven we should take our fingers off the keyboard, drop the cell phone, put away the vacuum cleaner, garage the lawn mower and go to church. Once there, we must put all those things out of our minds and focus exclusively on God.

The Sabbath is a day of *relaxation*. Our bodies and minds can only take so much input and stress. Overloading with 24/7 work will have devastating effects on our physical and mental state. God knows this since He made us.

The Sabbath is a day of *reliance*. Since we are not out actively seeking an income, we are trusting God to provide for us. Taking one day off shows our reliance on God to bless us the other six.

The Chick-Fil-A website explains their reason for being closed on Sundays. The idea began with Truett Cathy, the founder, who said working all the time left him exhausted. Since 1946, that has been their policy, one that runs against the seven-day-a-week standard restaurant philosophy. Truett Cathy, on his own website, has a five step recipe for success. Guess what number 5 is:

CLOSED ON SUNDAY: *I was not so committed to financial success that I was willing to abandon my principles and* *priorities. One of the most visible examples of this is our decision to close on Sunday. Our decision to close on Sunday was our way of honoring God and of directing our attention to things that mattered more than our business.*

Chick-fil-A is the only major fast-food restaurant chain to be closed on Sundays, one of the busiest days of the week in the restaurant business. Despite being closed on Sundays, Truett Cathy has led Chick-fil-A on an unparalleled record of 38 consecutive years of sales increases, with its core free-standing restaurants achieving higher sales per unit in six days (with shorter operating hours) than most major chains in the industry.[1]

For Truett Cathy, there is something more important than making money and certainly Chick-Fil-A has not suffered from bankruptcy. His reliance on God for the other six days has been blessed. Renew your feelings toward the Sabbath and see what God will do while you do nothing but praise the Lord.

TODAY'S 40 DAY CHALLENGES

Read: **Hebrews 4:1-11**

Pray: **Dear God, I need to take a break on the Sabbath and focus on you. By doing so I show that I…**

Do: **Take a break the next Sabbath day. If you work on Sundays, don't. Reflect, relax and rely.**

---

[1] http://www.truettcathy.com/about_recipe.asp

Day 16

40 Days with Moses

Parents

Honor your father and your mother, so that you may live long in the land the LORD your God is giving you. Exodus 20:12

One thing we all have in common—we all have a mother and father.

If you were abandoned, adopted or created in a test tube, you have a biological mother and father. Now whether that mother and father knew each other, cared for one another or are still together…that's a different story.

Hopefully, that mother and father took care of you, provided for you, instructed you, modeled living for you, and showed you what it meant to be a true believer in God.

But not all parents are perfect. Most kids will quickly tell you that. All parents deep down know that they could have done a better job. Parents live with a deep seated guilt that they caused a child's misdirection or poor habits. The responsibility of having children always appears much greater after the child is born and especially during graduation ceremonies and weddings when years of memories flood the parent's mind.

Think about it…God allowed a parent to be responsible for one of His own children. God said, "Here, I've created this human and I'm giving you the task of raising them and showing them the way to live." The parent, in turn, must sacrifice everything and raise that child in a Godly home.

The way a father fathers determines how a person understands God the Father. An absent father leads to one's belief that God is absent and doesn't care. A present, loving father helps one to see God as a loving, spiritual Father.

The Bible has a mixed roster of good and bad parents.

Noah was a good parent by rescuing his family, but a drunken episode led one son to be cursed.

Abraham was good towards Isaac, but the illegitimate Ishmael incident had ripple effects that the world is still suffering over.

Samuel was a great prophet, but raised two terrible, dishonest sons.

David was a man after God's own heart, but his family turned into a graphic, trashy soap opera.

Solomon had so many wives it's hard to imagine that he spent quality time at the park with his children, pushing hundreds of them on the swing set. (Interestingly, he wrote much of Proverbs that contain the best parental wisdom we can find.)

This commandment is not for the parent. It does not say, "Be a good father and mother." It says "Honor your father and your mother." The burden here falls on the child to obey. The child must do the honoring whether the parent is honorable or not.

For some, that's easy…no problem. For many, that's difficult. History may not reflect well on your parent, or your present situation is so dysfunctional that honoring is the furthest thing from your mind. Maybe you don't even know your parent.

Whatever the issue, the commandment tells us to renew our perspective on our parents and honor them. *Honor* means to respect and hold with high regard. There is no escape clause to this commandment. "Honor them if they were good to you" or "Honor them if they made you happy." It just says honor them because they are your parents.

The second part of the fifth commandment tells us a lot about why this commandment is so important. There appears to be a direct connection between honoring parents and long life. Hatred toward our parents creates an unhealthy attitude in our souls that can literally kill us at an early age.

You can also make a case from this commandment that honoring our parents is directly related to the strength of a nation, the land God has given you. As children rebel against their parents, the very moral fabric of a nation begins to unravel.

Again, no parent is perfect, but that is not to stop us from honoring them. This commandment may require forgiveness first then honor second.

If you're having difficulty thinking of anything to honor your parents for, begin with their biological contribution to your existence and work from there.

It's good for you to honor your parents—for your spiritual perspective, your physical health and for the stability of the nation.

TODAY'S 40 DAY CHALLENGES

Read: **Proverbs 1**

Pray: **Dear God, thank you for my parents, because…**

Do: **Write a note or call your parents. Tell them you love them. If they have passed away, write an undeliverable note to them.**

Day 17

40 Days with Moses

Murder

You shall not murder. Exodus 20:13

Don't kill people!
Okay, got it. Next commandment.
On the surface, this is the easiest commandment to uphold. As long as I am not directly related to the murder of an individual, I win. Of all the Ten Commandments, this one probably gets broken the least. Right?
There's a great line in the movie "True Lies." Helen (Jamie Lee Curtis) just discovered that her husband Harry (Arnold Schwarzenegger) was a spy.

Helen: Have you ever killed anyone?
Harry: Yeah, but they were all bad.

Murder, in the world's eyes, is justifiable as long as they had it coming.
Well, before we close the chapter and pat ourselves on the back for successfully overcoming this commandment, let's look at what Jesus said before we think of ourselves too highly.

"You have heard that it was said to the people long ago, 'Do not murder, and anyone who murders will be subject to judgment.' But I tell you that anyone who is angry with his brother will be subject to judgment. Again, anyone who says to his brother, 'Raca,' is answerable to the Sanhedrin. But anyone who says, 'You fool!' will be in danger of the fire of hell."
Matthew 6:21-22

Jesus changed the rules for murder from interrupting the physical flow of blood to one's heart to stopping the emotional flow of love from one's heart to another.

Hatred kills.

If we kill someone in our heart, we are guilty of murder. Now ALL of us are on death row.

If you call someone a fool (Raca – literally "empty headed") or any other hurtful term—jerk, dummy, stupid head, doofus, moron—you are guilty of murder.

If you gossip about someone to another person, you are an accomplice to murder because you've caused that person to hate the other.

"But what if I was just telling the truth about some idiotic thing they did!" Then question your motivation for sharing that information with another.

In an arrest, the officer always pats down the suspect to find the murder weapon and confiscate it. In light of this new thinking about commandment five, the murder weapons are our minds and our mouths.

We need a new way of thinking and talking about other people. But don't arrest yourself yet. Just because a tempting "hateful" bullet enters your thought chamber doesn't mean you're guilty of murder. Temptations come from Satan. We are not guilty until we agree with that temptation and pull the trigger. So if that tempting thought enters our mind, urging us to assassinate another person's character, pray for them instead. Thank God for them. It diffuses the ammunition, fizzles and misfires.

Starting today, stop your mouth from tearing down another person and spreading vicious gossip. Instead, communicate something edifying about them. Talk about their good qualities. Yes, your mom was right…if you can't say something nice about a person, say nothing at all.

We all have "bad" people in our lives who deserve what's coming to them, but it's not our job to judge them since we are far from perfect ourselves.

While we all have blood stains on our consciences for the things that we have said, we must stop our murderous rampage and begin renewing our thoughts about other people.

TODAY'S 40 DAY CHALLENGES

Read: Matthew 5:21-26, 38-48

Pray: Dear God, I am guilty of murder in your eyes. Please forgive me for the way I have assassinated the character of...

Do: Don't gossip about anyone! Stop every temptation to tear down the character of another. Make every word today edifying and uplifting about other people and not destructive.

Day 18

40 Days with Moses

Sex

You shall not commit adultery. Exodus 20:14

This commandment is a lot like the murder commandment. Most married folk read this one and say, "Well, I've never had an affair that led to sex so I'm good on this one."

Leave it to Jesus to spoil our self-righteous party.

"You have heard that it was said, 'Do not commit adultery.' But I tell you that anyone who looks at a woman lustfully has already committed adultery with her in his heart." Matthew 5:27-28

A common phrase used by guys who are eyeing women is this, "Hey, I can look as long as I don't touch!" Jesus says, "You can't look at or touch any women in a sexual manner." Jesus turned this from a physical offense to a mental offense.

Pharisees of Jesus' time used to walk with their heads down so they would never look at a woman and be tempted by her. This probably caused many "head-on" collisions between Pharisees and architectural columns.

Muslims tell their women to cover their bodies with burqas, sometimes with only their eyes exposed. Is this the solution to adultery?

A woman or a man cannot be punished for their beauty. It's not their fault that they are gorgeous. The problem is what we do with the image of their beauty in our minds. We can't cover our eyes or have others wrap themselves in aluminum foil.

Now before you singles decide to turn the page and say, "Well, I'm single I can do what I want since adultery deals with married people," the principles of this commandment apply to you too. Do not engage in sexual immorality.

Let's look at the scene. There you are, walking down the street, when all of a sudden a beautiful girl (for this story) walks by. You turn. You see her. Your eyes communicate her physical specs to your mind. Nice hair. Nice body. Nice smile. Pretty eyes. The information is calculated, analyzed and compared to previous data on other girls you have seen. The conclusion: This girl is beautiful!

So far this is merely an OPINION. Not everyone would think she's beautiful. You do. Nothing wrong here. God made beauty. You don't commit adultery by looking at a beautiful sunset or a beautiful horse. What's the problem with a beautiful girl?

Next a TEMPTATION enters your mind. A little voice suggests a sexual thought. "Hey, wouldn't you like to have sex with her?" or "What do you think she looks like naked?" At this point, you still have not sinned! Temptation is not sin. Jesus was tempted in the desert. Jesus did not sin. Many of us beat ourselves up over the temptations believing those are our thoughts. No, those are from Satan!

Once a temptation crosses your mind, stop it. Pray against it. Just say NO!

The sin…or the line that we cross… occurs when we ACT upon the temptation. We follow through with the temptation and begin to dwell in our minds on the temptation. We imagine what it would be like to have sex with her. We picture her naked and dwell upon the thought for too long.

Now it's a problem.

(And ladies/gals/girls, you're not off the hook here because you're female. Sexual temptation crosses gender lines. It's everybody's struggle.)

Leviticus 20 contains one of the weirdest and sickest lists of sexual immoralities you've ever seen. If you read it in mixed company, you are sure to blush. It brings sexual perversions to your mind you've never even thought of—don't have sex with your father's wife, daughter-in-law, his sister, his brother's wife, his aunt, an animal—it sounds like an episode of Jerry Springer!

The point is—don't have physical or mental sex with anyone outside of the person you are married to! Not with anyone in your neighborhood. Not with anyone on the Internet. Not with anyone in a movie. Not with anyone. The Bible wants to be clear on this.

You have no excuse. "But I'm a man…and men are sexual beings."

So was Jesus…

Today is the day to renew your thoughts of others, not treating them as sexual fantasies for your fulfillment, but as real people who God loves dearly.

TODAY'S 40 DAY CHALLENGES

Read: John 8:1-11

Pray: **Dear God, help me with my thought life. I am guilty of sexual immorality in the areas of…**

Do: **If you watch porn, stop. If you find yourselves fantasizing about the opposite sex, next time, pray for them before the thought becomes a sin. If you are deep into addictive behavior, contact a pastor or trusted Christian friend to help you along.**

Day 19

40 Days with Moses

Stealing

"You shall not steal." Exodus 20:15

    I remember entering our home as a child after the funeral of my grandmother. We were gone to Peoria Illinois for a week and when we returned we could see our back window had been pried open. Immediately, all of us ran into the house (obviously not thinking someone could be in there) to see what had happened and what was missing. Some clothes, meat and costume jewelry were gone.
    While the items were not especially valuable, what was really missing was a sense of security. We felt violated and vulnerable. Immediately we started lining up the suspects in our minds and accusing (probably falsely) others of robbery. As victims we suffered greatly, not only because of the monetary loss.
    God hates stealing because it hurts the person from whom something is stolen from.
    But stealing also hurts the stealer. I'm not talking about when they get caught, but the false sense of entitlement the robber begins to feel.
    The robber thinks he deserves someone else's items. Because of an inflated sense of self, the robber believes he or she is greater and more powerful than others.
    The robber loses their faith in God to provide, choosing to take from others instead of relying on God to supply all their needs.
    The robber adopts a weak work ethic. He justifies his stealing as work, forgetting that payment should be a deserved reward.

The robber also lives with guilt. Something inside him eats away at his conscience, telling the robber that his actions were wrong.

The robber's family suffers also. A story in Joshua 7 tells of Achan who kept some possessions after an attack on Jericho. The Israelites lost the next war and when they asked God what happened, He said there was sin in the tribe. The sin of one thief caused a lack of blessing for his family.

Robbers used to be portrayed in the media as men in black shirts, black pants, black shoes, with a black hat and a black mask on. This covered their deeds in the darkness of night. Darkness is a perfect symbol for the mindset of the robbery. Thieves don't like to be recognized or exposed.

However, today's thieves aren't so obvious to spot. They look like you and me. Stealing has become more high tech, occurring at home, at work and at church.

'Do not use dishonest standards when measuring length, weight or quantity. Use honest scales and honest weights, an honest ephah and an honest hin. I am the LORD your God, who brought you out of Egypt. Leviticus 19:35-36

Are you stealing from work? Are you giving an honest price for a fair amount of service?

Are you stealing from the government? Are your taxes honestly filled out?

Are you stealing from other businesses? If they mischarge you are you letting them know and returning the incorrect change?

Are you stealing from your family? How are you handling a loved one's estate or are you robbing your parents without them knowing it?

Are you stealing from God? Is He getting what He deserves in your tithe?

Once someone realizes they have been stealing, there is a two step process that follows.

One, admit your guilt to God.

Second, return what you stole to the person you stole it from.

Now you can renew your relationship with others, your family and God in an honest, new and fresh way.

Stealing not only hurts others, but it hurts you.

TODAY'S 40 DAY CHALLENGES

Read: Joshua 7

Pray: Dear God, I have stolen from others. I admit that have taken...

Do: Return whatever it was you stole.

Day 20

40 Days with Moses

Mouth

You shall not give false testimony against your neighbor. – Exodus 20:16

"Liar, liar, pants on fire."

What a strange saying. It's usually said to the accused liar as a sort of condemnation for lying. It wishes them a hellish moment as their favorite pair of slacks lights up in flames.

Or you could say, "May your trousers spontaneously combust, you bearer of false witness!" That's probably too long.

Lying and hell are eternally linked. The word "devil" comes from the word "diabolos" which means slanderer, deceiver or liar. It all started in the Garden of Eden when the devil told the biggest lie of all—"You're better than God."

It would probably make life easier if people caught on fire when they told a lie. Everything from salesmen to repairmen to insurance agents to preachers would light up and we would immediately know if they were telling a lie.

Pinocchio had that problem. His growing nose gave him away. His lies were as clear as the nose on his face. Good thing that doesn't happen to us. Our noses don't grow and our pants don't catch on fire when we lie, but the damage is still pretty extensive. Our tongues are matches that can do more damage than a brush fire.

Likewise the tongue is a small part of the body, but it makes great boasts. Consider what a great forest is set on fire by a small spark. The tongue also is a fire, a world of evil among the parts of the body. It corrupts the whole person, sets the whole course of his life on fire, and is itself set on fire by hell. James 3:5-6

Our ears cannot hurt others by what we hear. Our eyes do no damage to our neighbors. Likewise our nose is innocent. The most dangerous weapon on our face is the tongue. It can be fierce and merciless to people around us when it spreads lies and accusations to the world.

So, as long as I don't lie about others, I'm okay, right?

The Paparazzi are an interesting bunch. Their job is to take photographs of celebrities doing stupid things. As long as they don't change the photos or take the moment out of context, basically they are just telling the truth about the life of a celebrity. What's wrong with that?

The problem begins with the motivation. We too can spread "truths" about people, but with the intention to tear them down. Maybe it was something shared with us in private or a prayer request given in confidence. If we start passing around that truthful information to others, we must question our motivation. Is it for their edification or for my glorification?

Usually our intention for spreading falsehoods is to raise our own self-importance. Admit it, there is a certain "high" to the moment when we rip into someone, because we suddenly feel better about ourselves. Tear them down. Build me up. It's as if we're all a part of some great big self-esteem horse race. If I can keep you back, then I can stay ahead. By exposing your faults and maligning your actions, I can win.

Realistically, there is no race. If there is a crowd watching this shameful competition it's God and He knows all truth and all intentions. He just shakes his head as we all fight and claw to be on top.

Gossip, slander, rumor, hearsay, idle talk, ranting and murmuring must stop in the life of a person. Instead we should build each other up.

He died for us so that, whether we are awake or asleep, we may live together with him. Therefore encourage one another and build each other up, just as in fact you are doing. 1 Thessalonians 5:10-11

Examine every word that comes from your mouth and see if its purpose is to encourage and exhort another. If it's not, THEN KEEP YOUR MOUTH SHUT! Renew your speech by saying more positive and no negative.

Or you may need to buy a new pair of asbestos pants.

TODAY'S 40 DAY CHALLENGES

Read: **James 3**

Pray: **Dear God, my tongue is an arsonist. I have set many fires in the lives of others, especially…**

Do: **All week keep track of your speech. Are your words building up or tearing down? If it tears down another, make a promise that you will apologize to that person. If anything, that will act as a deterrent from you saying something negative.**

Day 21

40 Days with Moses

Coveting

"You shall not covet your neighbor's house. You shall not covet your neighbor's wife, or his manservant or maidservant, his ox or donkey, or anything that belongs to your neighbor." Exodus 20:17

I have never desired my neighbor's donkey. Coveting donkeys is not a problem I face on a daily basis. Why is that?

Well, because I don't want a donkey and my neighbor doesn't have a donkey.

While donkey-coveting is not a problem for many today, coveting everything else is. From this commandment we see the beginning of the old adage: the grass is always greener on the other side of the fence. Other people have more and better and I want it.

My sons cough and clear their throats when they see the latest video game system or the newest cell phone. They are always quick to point out what their friend just received, how many and how much. I too look at people driving new cars and sigh. We bought a great house, but it didn't take long until we walked through another house and saw ours in a new light.

Sometimes I desire a business to cut my lawn and clean my house. I heard the other day of a company that comes out and cleans up your dog's poop. Suddenly, I wanted that too.

As for our neighbor's wife…it's true, we see something really spectacular in another person's spouse and suddenly our spouse doesn't look so good. We'll find one thing good in another person and suddenly we see everything bad in our own spouse.

Coveting is a problem because it makes unfair comparisons. We must remember nobody is perfect, including us and our spouses and our neighbor and his/her spouse. Even their donkeys are not perfect.

We cannot rightfully say that just because our neighbor's wife is an excellent cook that my wife is a terrible woman. Or just because our neighbor's husband makes more money that my husband is loser. That wife may be a great cook, but a terrible listener. Or that husband may make more money, but works all the time, spending no time with the kids and forgetting "date nights."

Coveting leads to stealing and overspending. Thieves take because they want and feel they deserve. Over spenders rob themselves of money they don't have so they can keep up with others that do.

Coveting leaps to the conclusion that your life is unfulfilled. You feel God has done an inadequate job providing for you the things you need. It places the value of life into things. Unfortunately those things break, fall apart and, in a matter of a year, are out of style. It's a deep hole you can never fill.

God referenced this commandment to a neighbor, because a neighbor traditionally was the one person you were in contact with on a daily basis. Today, we rarely see our neighbors, but we do watch TV and go on the Internet. "Neighbor" now applies to all those we see in commercials and on TV shows.

God commands us to stop desiring other people's houses, their spouses, their hired help, their possessions (animals and livestock back then, car and lawn mower today) or anything at all that they own.

Just because your neighbor has something you don't, it doesn't mean his life is perfect. He has his own problems and is probably looking over the fence at your life.

We must remember that we are blessed. If you are reading this book, you have more money than billions on this earth would ever dream. Go to another country and see for yourself. I saw a home in Cuba that hung a hubcap on the wall as decoration. Another had McDonald Happy Meal toys on their shelves, which they considered priceless figurines from a far away land.

Remember that more does not make you happier. More means more bills, more maintenance, and more complications.

To combat coveting, we must be thankful for what we have. It may not be perfect or the latest style, but we have *something* and that something has been given to us from God. Coveting forgets that God is that giver and it accuses Him of mismanaging that giving.

God never makes a mistake. You have what you are supposed to have.

Renew your appreciation for your possessions and look at them as gifts from God. That includes your donkey.

TODAY'S 40 DAY CHALLENGES

Read: 2 Samuel 11 – David coveted his neighbor's wife. See how much trouble he got into.

Pray: Dear God, my eyes wander and desire what others have. It makes me discontent and unsatisfied. Lord, I must thank you for giving me...

Do: Go to www.globalrichlist.com and see how your income compares to the income of everyone in the world. Do you have more than you think?

Day 22

40 Days with Moses

Remembering

When the people saw that Moses was so long in coming down from the mountain, they gathered around Aaron and said, "Come, make us gods who will go before us. As for this fellow Moses who brought us up out of Egypt, we don't know what has happened to him."
Aaron answered them, "Take off the gold earrings that your wives, your sons and your daughters are wearing, and bring them to me." So all the people took off their earrings and brought them to Aaron. He took what they handed him and made it into an idol cast in the shape of a calf, fashioning it with a tool. Then they said, "These are your gods, O Israel, who brought you up out of Egypt."
When Aaron saw this, he built an altar in front of the calf and announced, "Tomorrow there will be a festival to the LORD." So the next day the people rose early and sacrificed burnt offerings and presented fellowship offerings. Afterward they sat down to eat and drink and got up to indulge in revelry.
Then the LORD said to Moses, "Go down, because your people, whom you brought up out of Egypt, have become corrupt. They have been quick to turn away from what I commanded them and have made themselves an idol cast in the shape of a calf. They have bowed down to it and sacrificed to it and have said, 'These are your gods, O Israel, who brought you up out of Egypt.' Exodus 32:1-8

For 40 days, while all went well up on the mountain, things fell apart down below. What happened? It's not like the Israelites didn't have any proof for the existence of God.

Before them stood Mount Horeb, all ablaze with God's presence—smoke, clouds and lightning. Quite a show.

Then, during those 40 days, everyone lost hope of seeing Moses again and began to worship other gods. They made a golden calf. Why a golden calf?

The golden calf was a symbol of their past life in Egypt. Egyptians worshipped all kinds of animals. We see cows worshipped in the Hindu faith today. Horoscopes include Taurus the bull. Cow worshipping is not new. Cows give milk and meat, which give life, so the worshipping of a cow was done because the Israelites believed they would get sustenance and life from it.

For some reason, the Israelites thought that worshipping an idol would make a lot of sense. The calf was a safer god to worship. It did not have the powerful, teeth-chattering presence like the God they saw on that mountain. The calf was more approachable. Heck they made it with their own hands. They were the god of the handmade god!

The calf required very little from their lives. Not all these 10 Commandments! And the Book of Leviticus! Wow, that's asking a lot. The calf required some sacrifices and a festival now and then. Eating and drinking. More like a party. Who doesn't like a party?

To create the idol, the Israelites had to give up a lot—their possessions, their gold earrings, their time to make the idol. They also gave up their faith in God.

But it was their short term memory lapse that caused the idol worship. God had just shown them a spectacular rescue in Egypt. Then, just like that, it was a distant memory. The calf was here and now. They could see it and touch it, even though it had no power.

Forgetting always causes a slide away from God. That's why, through the rest of the Bible, the rescue from Egypt was recounted and remembered over and over so the people would not forget what God had done for them.

Today we lose our faith in God and give up on Him too. Why? We forget what He has done. By remembering the great things He has done, we gain hope for the great things *He will do*. Just because God appears to be missing, don't believe He has forgotten you or He doesn't care any longer.

If He *was* a God who cared, then He *is* a God who cares.

Take the time to remember God's past interventions in your life and the way He walked you through difficult times. Renew your faith by remembering the memories.

Any other thoughts are just a lot of bull.

TODAY'S 40 DAY CHALLENGES

Read: **Psalm 42**

Pray: **Dear God, I remember all the times you have been there for me and helped me when I needed you most. Like...**

Do: **Write down five times God has intervened and helped you in the past.**

Day 23

40 Days with Moses

Responsibility

When Moses approached the camp and saw the calf and the dancing, his anger burned and he threw the tablets out of his hands, breaking them to pieces at the foot of the mountain. And he took the calf they had made and burned it in the fire; then he ground it to powder, scattered it on the water and made the Israelites drink it.

He said to Aaron, "What did these people do to you, that you led them into such great sin?"

"Do not be angry, my lord," Aaron answered. "You know how prone these people are to evil. They said to me, 'Make us gods who will go before us. As for this fellow Moses who brought us up out of Egypt, we don't know what has happened to him.' So I told them, 'Whoever has any gold jewelry, take it off.' Then they gave me the gold, and I threw it into the fire, and out came this calf!"

Moses saw that the people were running wild and that Aaron had let them get out of control and so become a laughingstock to their enemies. Exodus 32:19-25

What a way to come home after a fabulous 40 day retreat with God. When Moses stepped off the mountain after his time with God, he found the Israelites worshipping the golden calf. While some of the blame pointed to the people, we must not forget who was in charge—Aaron, Moses' brother.

Aaron first became part of the Israeli Rescue Team because of his speaking abilities, however he sorely lacked in his leadership qualities. What did Aaron do wrong?

First, he blamed the people. Aaron called them "evil." Their request to make gods sounded threatening, as if Aaron felt his life was in danger.

Second, Aaron caved in. He implicates himself by asking them to take off their gold jewelry to make this idol. Aaron actively participated in the scheme.

Finally, Aaron outright lied. Did he really throw the gold in the fire and a calf came out? If that's the case, then this god should be worshipped because that was a miracle!

Aaron should have taken responsibility for what happened right from the beginning. A simple explanation and apology would suffice. Obviously Aaron was afraid and immediately knew he had broken a brand new fresh law about worshipping idols (it didn't take long, did it), making him look even dumber as he piled lie upon lie. Sure the people were to blame, but they would be held accountable for their own sin.

Aaron should have stood strong. When the people begged for an idol, Aaron should have replied, "NO!" He feared for his own reputation and not God's reputation. As a result, the entire nation became a laughingstock to their enemies (word travels fast).

Aaron should have told the truth. His lie only made it worse and less plausible. His lie even blamed God for the calf. Since the mysteriously created calf was "a miracle" and God is God of miracles, Aaron's lie pointed to God as the creator of a god. Big mistake, but probably not his intention.

During our time of renewal, we must examine how we handle our mistakes.

Do we take responsibility for our actions?
Do we stand strong in the face of opposition?
Do we tell the truth?

One of humanity's favorite pastimes is the Blame Game. The rules: make a mistake, then point your finger at as many people and objects as you can. Extra points if you blame God!

Obviously this game has no winner and it just makes the participants look dumb.

Once we take responsibility, we can begin a process of repentance and healing. Blame only delays the process.

It's true—everyone makes mistakes. But, not everyone accepts responsibility for those mistakes and asks God for forgiveness.

Renew your responsibility for your actions by first examining yourself.

TODAY'S 40 DAY CHALLENGES

Read: **2 Samuel 12 – see how David handled his mistakes**

Pray: **Dear God, is it my fault? If so, forgive me. I'm the one who…**

Do: **Write down two things you blame others for, but from now on, you need to take responsibility.**

Day 24

40 Days with Moses

Fasting

When I went up on the mountain to receive the tablets of stone, the tablets of the covenant that the LORD had made with you, I stayed on the mountain forty days and forty nights; I ate no bread and drank no water. The LORD gave me two stone tablets inscribed by the finger of God. On them were all the commandments the LORD proclaimed to you on the mountain out of the fire, on the day of the assembly... Then once again I fell prostrate before the LORD for forty days and forty nights; I ate no bread and drank no water, because of all the sin you had committed, doing what was evil in the LORD's sight and so provoking him to anger. Deuteronomy 9:9-10, 18

    We all like food. We like good food. Food and good go together. Food and good look like they should rhyme, since they both end in "ood." They don't rhyme, but they are still a wonderful match. Either way, food brings goodness and satisfaction to us.

    Water is a necessary component for existence. You can live weeks without food, but only days without water. Water comprises over fifty percent of our body. Water really is life.

    Moses ascended that mountain and held TWO conferences with God. The first occurred BC (Before Calf) and the second occurred AD (After Destruction of calf). Each time he fell before the Lord in a prostrate position and did not eat or drink water for the entire time. How could he do that?

    Not eating and drinking water for forty days is not recommended unless you are in the presence of the Lord. God miraculously took care of Moses physically (as He did

Jesus in the desert, which we'll see later). You should only engage in that kind of fast if God directs you to.

What's also amazing about this story is that Moses chose not to eat or drink. He was so engaged in the time with God and with the responsibility that lay before him, Moses did not consider eating as a high priority.

Eating is our priority. The idea of eating comes to mind, it seems, every half hour. However, it's funny, when we're really engaged in some duty or conversation, time flies and the next thing we know, our minds haven't thought about eating.

Do you notice how you eat more when you're bored or watching TV? Food acts as a stimulus to keep you awake.

Moses found something so important, so heartbreaking, so engaging, so pressing that his own physical well-being took a back seat. He would rather pray than eat.

We must ask ourselves—what is it that's so important to us that we would be willing to skip a meal or two or twenty-two? Sometimes we allow those important matters to slip away or we just give up and figure they will never get any better. We turn to our needs instead and fill our own mouths while others go starving for God's blessing.

What keeps you up at night? What brings tears to your eyes? What causes you to shake your head and say, "something must be done"?

Is it getting the good news of Jesus Christ into the world? Or maybe getting salvation to the heart of a loved one? People are dying without God. What do you think about that?

Is the future of this nation bothering you?

How's your neighbor? How about your co-worker's life choices? Or maybe the direction your child is headed?

Does a teeter-tottering relationship make you uneasy? What about your children? Your spouse?

What about the state of our schools, our culture, our community, the world?

How about your church? Is it transforming people's lives?

Does anything bother you or are you just filling your own mouth?

Moses ached for God's people. It really tore him up. His perspective shifted from self to others. We need that perspective shift too. Fasting reveals that shift. We need to find something outside of ourselves that commands our attention, our soul and our time.

We must be willing to renew our passion for spiritual matters and go without a meal now and then so we can spend more time praying and less time consuming.

TODAY'S 40 DAY CHALLENGES

Read: **Esther 4**

Pray: **Dear God, I've been too worried about myself. My heart breaks for...**

Do: **What is the one thing that you would like to see happen? Have you considered fasting for one meal, one day or three days and praying instead of eating?**

Day 25

40 Days with Moses

Intercession

I lay prostrate before the LORD those forty days and forty nights because the LORD had said he would destroy you. I prayed to the LORD and said, "O Sovereign LORD, do not destroy your people, your own inheritance that you redeemed by your great power and brought out of Egypt with a mighty hand. Remember your servants Abraham, Isaac and Jacob. Overlook the stubbornness of this people, their wickedness and their sin. Otherwise, the country from which you brought us will say, 'Because the LORD was not able to take them into the land he had promised them, and because he hated them, he brought them out to put them to death in the desert.' But they are your people, your inheritance that you brought out by your great power and your outstretched arm."
Deuteronomy 9:25-29

Secret Service Agents fascinate me. First of all, it's the title "Secret" that's cool. However, you can always spot them around the President—the large, unhappy guys with dark sunglasses, wearing suits with large bulges around their chest pockets. Their job takes them along with the President of the United States, who creates tense moments wherever he goes. They are always on duty, scanning the crowds, watching for danger, profiling and analyzing people's eyes, actions and packages.

When Presidents Kennedy, Reagan and Ford were shot at, the Secret Service went into action. Within seconds, they surrounded the President, ready to take a bullet for him. Tim McCarthy, the agent with Reagan at the time, did just that and got shot in the stomach. Within three seconds, the assassin John Hinckley fired six shots, but within a second, the Secret Service saved Reagan's life.

Moses could be considered a sort of Secret Service Agent. When the Israelites' sin caused God to pull out his weapon, threatening to take the nation out, Moses stepped in the path. Now the Israelites deserved God's judgment, so the scenario is different from a presidential assassination, but the concept of a person stepping out and protecting another from harm is very biblical.

It's called "interceding" and it occurs on a spiritual level. Moses interceded for his people. Interceding means stepping between two parties and speaking up for them when they cannot fully do so themselves. If someone is weakened by the emotional strain of divorce, or the desperation of a death or the trauma of a career failure, another friend steps up and steps in and prays the prayers of protection, strength and encouragement for that person.

God cannot be pushed around, but He will listen to our case. Moses reminded God that He was sovereign. He mentioned the promise of creating a great nation with these people and the impact it would have on the other nations. Moses pleaded for mercy and fell on his face for another 40 days and 40 nights.

Moses' argument wasn't eloquent or unique. God didn't feel sorry for his decision or embarrassed for Moses. What impressed God was Moses' willingness to stand up for another—to literally lie on his face for 40 days.

Who around you is suffering through a difficult time? What are you willing to do for them? Just a casual prayer before you lay on your back for seven hours and go to sleep? Or could you take the time hour after hour, day in and day out to intercede for them?

Think of the encouragement they would receive after hearing of your decision to intercede for them in prayer.

During these 40 Days, keep your eyes open for people who seriously need prayer. Renew your attitude toward them and be willing to intercede for them, even if it means taking a few spiritual bullets in your heart.

TODAY'S 40 DAY CHALLENGES

Read: **Romans 8:26-27**

Pray: **Dear God, I know of someone who is hurting. I want to intercede for them. Please be with...**

Do: **Call that person who is suffering and offer to pray with them, in person or on the phone.**

Day 26

40 Days with Moses

Again

Now I had stayed on the mountain forty days and nights, as I did the first time, and the LORD listened to me at this time also. It was not his will to destroy you. "Go," the LORD said to me, "and lead the people on their way, so that they may enter and possess the land that I swore to their fathers to give them." Deuteronomy 10:10-11

"Do-over." The words mean start again. Sometimes it's a good thing. You get to correct the mistakes of the past. Other times it's a bad thing. All that work for nothing. Just a waste of time.

Personally I hate do-overs. I like to get it right the first time. I especially hate the do-overs that occur because of power outages and computer freezes. All that writing and creative thought gone because of an electronic glitch.

I have found one thing with do-overs—the second time is usually better. I hate to admit that, but erasing the slate and starting again gives me a fresh perspective on a problem area. Second drafts, as painful as they are to write, do come out smoother and fresher. Why? Because we try to solve problems in the middle of the situation, which is sometimes surrounded by problems on both sides. We should instead start over at the beginning, set it up correctly with the problems clearly in view, make changes along the way and re-create the situation in a problem-free environment.

We remember that Moses went up the mountain for 40 days and 40 nights, but did you know before you started reading this devotion that he went back up for another 40 days and 40 nights?

A mountain top do-over. 40 Days Part II. Was it necessary again? God has done do-overs before. Remember Noah? God did a do-over with human civilization. Things were better the second time, but not perfect.

After Moses' second 40 days on the mountain, God sent the Israelites on their way toward the Promised Land. He felt they were ready. It took not one, but two 40 day periods to get it right. Was the first one a waste of time?

Not at all. Moses received the law the first time. The legal groundwork was established during that period. It also exposed the weaknesses in the people and the leadership. Moses came down from the mountain, threw the tablets in anger and lost control. The Israelites saw their own lack of faith in the idol making. They needed to stop being distracted by the idols of the past.

The second time around, the Israelites certainly could not be considered perfect people, but they were definitely better and more ready to receive God's blessing and God's tasks for their lives.

Moses also showed God the second time that he was more serious about the task that lay before him. By committing to another 40 days, food-free and on his face, Moses proved he was God's man. God loved his dedication and rewarded him with renewed responsibility.

Renewal is not a one time thing and that's that. You won't find many saying, "Hey, I got renewed the first time! I'm perfect!"

Renewal requires us to go back to God over and over again. Why? Things change. God doesn't change but we do, as well as our circumstances and the people around us.

We may need to renew and re-renew the way we react toward situations and others.

Our circumstances grow more difficult and we need to seek a renewed strength to deal with them.

Those around us change their minds, go off-course or sin, affecting us and our situation.

This 40 Day process you are journeying through will definitely be worth it, but it won't solve all of your problems just like that. Things change and you may need to go back to the Lord again for another 40 Day experience.

So, make sure you get it right this time and take care of as many mistakes as you can. That way the second time will be much easier.

TODAY'S 40 DAY CHALLENGES

Read: **Colossians 3:1-17**

Pray: **Dear God, I know that I'm not perfect and I must continue to seek renewal with you all the time. I pray this time you help me face the issue of...**

Do: **Read this section a second time. Did you learn something different?**

Day 27

40 Days with Moses

Glow

When Moses came down from Mount Sinai with the two tablets of the Testimony in his hands, he was not aware that his face was radiant because he had spoken with the LORD. When Aaron and all the Israelites saw Moses, his face was radiant, and they were afraid to come near him. But Moses called to them; so Aaron and all the leaders of the community came back to him, and he spoke to them. Afterward all the Israelites came near him, and he gave them all the commands the LORD had given him on Mount Sinai. When Moses finished speaking to them, he put a veil over his face. But whenever he entered the LORD's presence to speak with him, he removed the veil until he came out. And when he came out and told the Israelites what he had been commanded, they saw that his face was radiant. Then Moses would put the veil back over his face until he went in to speak with the LORD. Exodus 34:29-35

Do you glow?
There are all sorts of moments that cause a glow. Brides glow. So do parents of a newborn. Graduates glow upon receiving their diploma.

Light bulbs have an external, transparent casing with an internal filament. That filament gets red hot and it glows. It shines through the glass casing, which is there to protect the filament from getting busted.

We are like those bulbs. Inside all believers the Holy Spirit shines. He radiates with God's love and the joy of salvation. It's His heart glowing for the world through us and drawing others to come into a saving relationship with Jesus

Christ. However, many who see us do not detect a glow. Why?

Our external casing blocks the light. I'm not talking about our skin, muscle and bones. Our "transparency" is directly related to our attitudes, moods and negativity. These "blockers" dim our light, making it difficult for the glow to shine through us.

While many of us want to blame our circumstances or others for our lack of transparency, the truth is we control how transparent we are. Like the saying goes, people can affect your situation but they can't affect how you respond to the situation. That's within our control.

The Holy Spirit is not on a dimmer. God shines at one consistent level.

"You are the light of the world. A city on a hill cannot be hidden. Neither do people light a lamp and put it under a bowl. Instead they put it on its stand, and it gives light to everyone in the house. In the same way, let your light shine before men, that they may see your good deeds and praise your Father in heaven." Matthew 5:14-16

Notice Jesus does not talk about us putting out the light. Instead, we smother it or hide it. Under that bowl covering, the light will still shine. Removing the bowl makes it effective.

Moses departed from his 40 Day mountain-top experience literally glowing. It was a spiritual tan that would make George Hamilton blush (if he could).

Spending time with God removes the layers that make us opaque. It gives us perspective on God's power and His purpose and strips our external blockers. Our mood lightens because we know God loves us. Our attitude shifts because we see our final destination. Negativity turns positive as we understand the joy of the Lord.

How radiant are you? What is preventing God's light from shining through you?

Renew your spirit, then go and glow.

TODAY'S 40 DAY CHALLENGES

Read: Psalm 80

Pray: **Dear God, I want to radiate with your Holy Spirit. I want people to know through my life and my words and my actions that I have a relationship with you. Help me to…**

Do: **Write down five things that can adjust your transparency (those blockers). Now that you've recognized them, don't let them keep the Holy Spirit from shining through you.**

Day 28

40 Days with Joshua & Caleb

Promises

At the end of forty days they returned from exploring the land. They came back to Moses and Aaron and the whole Israelite community at Kadesh in the Desert of Paran. There they reported to them and to the whole assembly and showed them the fruit of the land. They gave Moses this account: "We went into the land to which you sent us, and it does flow with milk and honey! Here is its fruit. But the people who live there are powerful, and the cities are fortified and very large. We even saw descendants of Anak there. The Amalekites live in the Negev; the Hittites, Jebusites and Amorites live in the hill country; and the Canaanites live near the sea and along the Jordan." Then Caleb silenced the people before Moses and said, "We should go up and take possession of the land, for we can certainly do it." Numbers 13:25-30

After receiving the commandments from the Lord, Moses led the nation to the border of their new home, the Promised Land, shown to Abraham by God. Moses sent twelve spies into the land, one from each tribe, including Joshua (Hoshea) from Ephraim and Caleb from Judah. They were in the land for 40 days and returned with a report. What did they see during that time?

Great blessings and great obstacles.

Every spy agreed that the land was beautiful and plentiful, compared to the desert region of Egypt they just crossed. In comparison, this was paradise. The closest to the Garden of Eden they had ever seen on earth. Gorgeous scenery, fertile ground, plump fruit. They all wanted to live there. And who wouldn't? Obviously others saw and enjoyed the beauty of Israel too. A place like that doesn't sit undiscovered for long. So while they were living and suffering in Egypt, someone else took over in the land promised to Abraham.

However, the spies disagreed on their perspective of the enemy that inhabited the land. All twelve could tell that these people were big and mean in a physical sense. Only two saw them as weak in a spiritual sense.

For those 40 days, twelve spies entered the assignment confident and assured, but ten returned frightened and discouraged. They all saw the same thing. What did Joshua and Caleb experience that the others didn't?

Joshua and Caleb saw both the great blessing and the great obstacle but remembered the promise. God said before they left:

"Send some men to explore the land of Canaan, which I am giving to the Israelites..." Numbers 13:2

God promised to give them the land. Ten spies saw giant warriors that were bigger than God. Two spies saw puny sticks that God would snap...somehow...some way...

If you forget the promise, you won't get the blessing and the obstacles will take you down every time.

What are the promises God offers us today? Well that would take another book, but generally God promises to love us (1 John 4:7-12, John 15), to forgive us (1 John 1:9, Psalm 103:12), to save us (John 3:16, Romans 10:9), to provide for us (Matthew 6), to be our sufficiency (Philippians 4), to watch over us (1 Peter 3:12-13, John 10:27-29)...the list goes on.

You can't face the obstacles that surround the blessing unless you remember the promises. You can only remember the promises if you meditate, memorize and read them. Every chapter of the Bible contains some sort of promise from God. The entire book is a promise of God's faithfulness.

If you don't want to be frightened by the obstacles any longer, remember the promises and believe them. All twelve spies heard the promise. Only Joshua and Caleb believed it during those 40 days. A promise is only as solid as the one giving the promise. So the bigger question is this: do you trust God, the promise maker?

If you renew your trust in God, the giants you face suddenly seem much smaller.

TODAY'S 40 DAY CHALLENGES

Read: **Open up the Bible and read one of the promise verses mentioned in the devotion.**

Pray: **Dear God, I have heard the promises. Now I must ask if I truly believe them. When it comes to your promises, I...**

Do: **Memorize a verse with a promise. Keep it on a card with you all day. Don't let go of it!**

Day 29

40 Days with David

Story

Goliath stood and shouted to the ranks of Israel, "Why do you come out and line up for battle? Am I not a Philistine, and are you not the servants of Saul? Choose a man and have him come down to me. If he is able to fight and kill me, we will become your subjects; but if I overcome him and kill him, you will become our subjects and serve us." Then the Philistine said, "This day I defy the ranks of Israel! Give me a man and let us fight each other." On hearing the Philistine's words, Saul and all the Israelites were dismayed and terrified...For forty days the Philistine came forward every morning and evening and took his stand. 1 Samuel 17:8-11, 16

    A good film always shows someone overcoming the odds. The hero is up against a powerful force and in the process, the fate of the world, his relationship with the girl and his life all hang in the balance. In the meantime, he's been shot in the shoulder, his car blew up, all his money is gone, he ran out of bullets and his dog is missing.

    But if the hero had everything at his disposal and all the odds were in his favor, the enemy never had a chance and, as a result, the story is a yawner.

    The story of David versus Goliath is a story of an underdog taking on a much bigger, much meaner enemy. It begins with David, the runt of the family, a poor little shepherd boy, going to deliver lunch to his big brothers and finds them stuck in a stalemate with the Philistines in the Valley of Elah.

    For 40 days, Goliath taunted the armies and the Bible says the army ran away every time he stepped out. David heard those taunts and couldn't believe his ears. Look what David was up against.

Goliath. A seven-to-nine foot tall monster. Yao Ming with Hulk Hogan muscles. Goliath was confident and had the armor to protect him. Impressive and cocky. The kind of villain you always want to see fall in the end.

David's family. When David questioned the armies' cowardice, his brothers got mad at him. "You're just a shepherd and our lunch cart. Don't insult us."

The king. David went to the king Saul and offered to take care of the situation. Saul denied his first request.

The armor. Every soldier wears standard protection. A helmet for the head. A breast plate for the heart. However, it didn't come in David's size. He entered the battle practically naked.

Weaponry. Goliath had the latest, greatest and biggest spear you could find. David had an everyday rock.

Shield bearer. Goliath had back-up. Never mind he was twice the size of David, but he had help too. Two against one. Uneven odds.

Doesn't seem like a fair fight? Actually, you're right. Goliath didn't have a chance. David had a secret weapon and it wasn't his five smooth stones and incredible accuracy.

David said to the Philistine, "You come against me with sword and spear and javelin, but I come against you in the name of the LORD Almighty, the God of the armies of Israel, whom you have defied. This day the LORD will hand you over to me, and I'll strike you down and cut off your head. Today I will give the carcasses of the Philistine army to the birds of the air and the beasts of the earth, and the whole world will know that there is a God in Israel. All those gathered here will know that it is not by sword or spear that the LORD saves; for the battle is the LORD's, and he will give all of you into our hands." 1 Samuel 17:45-47

This is the classic story of the underdog triumphing over the giant. What separates the hero from the victims is what occurred for those 40 days of taunting. Every soldier had the opportunity to become the hero, but they all ran. They all knew something needed to be done, but only David did something about it.

There is probably a force taunting you during these 40 Days, calling you names, making you feel small. It may be a co-worker, classmate or a family member. You may have all the resources you need, but none of it works for you.

Whatever the odds, you have the opportunity to write a great story about your situation. You have a very powerful secret weapon—your strength and faith in the Lord.

Renew your strength. Renew your shield. Renew your faith.

Nothing can stop you now.

Write the story. Be the hero. Not the coward.

TODAY'S 40 DAY CHALLENGES

Read: 1 Samuel 17

Pray Dear God, I am in a battle. The odds are against me. I cannot win this battle alone unless...

Do: David remembered times when God saved him from lions and bears. Can you think of times in the past when God saved you too?

Day 30

40 Days with Elijah

Future

Elijah was afraid and ran for his life. When he came to Beersheba in Judah, he left his servant there, while he himself went a day's journey into the desert. He came to a broom tree, sat down under it and prayed that he might die. "I have had enough, LORD," he said. "Take my life; I am no better than my ancestors." Then he lay down under the tree and fell asleep. All at once an angel touched him and said, "Get up and eat." He looked around, and there by his head was a cake of bread baked over hot coals, and a jar of water. He ate and drank and then lay down again. The angel of the LORD came back a second time and touched him and said, "Get up and eat, for the journey is too much for you." So he got up and ate and drank. Strengthened by that food, he traveled forty days and forty nights until he reached Horeb, the mountain of God. There he went into a cave and spent the night. 1 Kings 19:3-9

  Elijah was God's prophet called to speak out against one of Israel's worst leaders—King Ahab. Ahab led the northern nation of Israel for 23 years during a period in the post-Solomon civil war. During that time he worshipped the god Baal and married an evil wife, Jezebel. Jezebel made sport of God's prophets and killed them off, one by one.

  Elijah countered her attack with a spectacular lightning show on Mount Carmel which led to the slaughter of 450 prophets of Baal. Jezebel was a little ticked off and posted a death threat on Elijah. The story picks up at 1 Kings 19. Depressed and on the run, Elijah hit the road, running all

the way back to the wilderness where Moses wandered with the Israelites for 40 years.
What happened to Elijah during that post-victory period? It should have been a celebration. Instead it turned into a pity party. For 40 days Elijah could have dwelled on God's victory, but he chose to dwell on what he thought was his dismal future.
Two times an angel tried to kick-start him. Finally, Elijah got up, more annoyed if anything by the persistent angel.
Elijah showed up at a place familiar with us these 40 days—Mount Horeb, the mountain where God gave Moses the Law and Ten Commandments (see Deuteronomy 5). This location reminded Elijah of God's faithfulness and promise.
But Elijah missed the meaning. Instead of standing on the mountain where Moses talked to God, he hid in a cave. Finally, God spoke to Elijah and told him to get up on the mountain. Elijah stood on the mountain and God asked a very penetrating questions: "What are you doing here?"

He replied, "I have been very zealous for the LORD God Almighty. The Israelites have rejected your covenant, broken down your altars, and put your prophets to death with the sword. I am the only one left, and now they are trying to kill me too." 1 Kings 19:14

God must given one of those disappointing sighs (that's from my translation), then handed Elijah three final tasks—anoint two kings (God's way of political election) and Elijah's successor, Elisha. Elijah had been downsized. A demotion. Elijah was no longer "the only one," as he called himself. Why?
Because for 40 days Elijah feared the future and forgot the past. He felt alone. He worried over something he knew nothing about. He forgot that God was still at work. God told Elijah that He had 7,000 more followers, all pure and undefiled like Elijah.

By forgetting the past—the victories of God and His promises—Elijah gave up, there on the very mountain where God made great promises and fulfilled them! God never gave up before, why would He give up now?

But a prophet without vision is of no profit to God. Their whole job is about trusting God and His promises for the future. So Elijah passed the mantle to his successor, trained him on the job, and then departed in a glorious heavenly taxi.

If you want to be useful today, get out of the cave of your past and climb to the top of the mountain to renew your commitment to God's future. God has something to show you.

Do it before someone takes your place.

TODAY'S 40 DAY CHALLENGES

Read: 1 Kings 19:19-21 – read Elisha's response

Pray: **Dear God, I keep looking back instead of looking forward. As I result I feel…**

Do: **Write down three things from the past that keep holding you back. Then write down three promises God has given you for the future. Which should you dwell on more?**

Day 31

40 Days with Ezekiel

Sin

"Then lie on your left side and put the sin of the house of Israel upon yourself. You are to bear their sin for the number of days you lie on your side. I have assigned you the same number of days as the years of their sin. So for 390 days you will bear the sin of the house of Israel. After you have finished this, lie down again, this time on your right side, and bear the sin of the house of Judah. I have assigned you 40 days, a day for each year. Turn your face toward the siege of Jerusalem and with bared arm prophesy against her. I will tie you up with ropes so that you cannot turn from one side to the other until you have finished the days of your siege." Ezekiel 4:4-8

In one of the most bizarre requests God ever gave a prophet, He asked Ezekiel to lie on his side and prophesy towards a miniature model of Jerusalem for 40 days (this after lying 390 days on his other side). Ezekiel obeyed and willingly allowed himself to be tied up. During that time, God revealed His plan for Israel and Judah (the two nations split by civil war).

Why such a drastic display that appears to be a waste of time? Why spend 40 days (and 390 days) lying around in the dirt and staring at a toy model?

This act was done out in the open so people passed by every day for over a year and saw the prophet lying on his side and speaking against their city. They certainly got the message.

Ezekiel not only communicated the message of the nations' destruction, he experienced their pain and isolation firsthand. While it was only a day for each year of isolation that the nations would experience, it still spoke volumes to him.

This was such a drastic request because sin is a drastic thing. Sin caused the separation of God and man. Sin divided a great nation. Sin turned hearts away from God and towards idols. Because of the destructiveness of sin, God hates it!

We forget that. We think God does not prefer sin or finds it an annoyance or shakes his head over sin. No, GOD HATES SIN!

Sin destroyed His great creation. Sin divided His heavenly ranks. Sin broke promises. Sin split relationships. Sin killed and sent His loved ones far away, where God will never see them again. GOD HATES SIN!

By the end of these 40 days, Ezekiel hated sin too. Sin caused him to lay bound up on the ground, cut off from his relationships, and separated from the ones he loved. He had time to ponder the destructiveness of sin.

What are your feelings toward sin? Mild annoyance? Unhealthy habit? Just the way it is? Or do you despise it?

It's not until we hate sin—seeing it for all its dreadful consequences—that we will choose not to engage in it any longer. We must hate sin as much as God hates sin. Only then we will seek holiness.

In this chapter, God calls Ezekiel the "son of man." It's the title Jesus chose for himself. Jesus too hated sin. Jesus also obediently followed God's direction and experienced sin firsthand, allowing Himself to be nailed to a cross and taking on the burden of the world's sin placed on His shoulders. While it was for only a few hours, it was far more painful than lying on your side for 40 days.

The drastic measures God takes in communicating His abhorrence of sin should tell us something. God hates sin and so should we. Only by understanding its consequences will His word change in our hearts. Renew your perspective on sin and hate it for all its worth.

Then thank God He doesn't ask you to lie on your side for 40 days to prove it.

TODAY'S 40 DAY CHALLENGES

Read: Ezekiel 5

Pray: Dear God, I have become too casual toward sin. I hate the fact that I...

Do: Lie down on your side (on the floor if you can) for ten minutes and confess your sins. Don't move.

Day 32

40 Days with Jonah

God's Word

Then the word of the LORD came to Jonah a second time: "Go to the great city of Nineveh and proclaim to it the message I give you." Jonah obeyed the word of the LORD and went to Nineveh. Now Nineveh was a very important city—a visit required three days. On the first day, Jonah started into the city. He proclaimed: "Forty more days and Nineveh will be overturned." The Ninevites believed God. They declared a fast, and all of them, from the greatest to the least, put on sackcloth. Jonah 3:1-5

     The Jonah story is about a reluctant prophet. Jonah didn't like the Ninevites and didn't want them to receive God's prophecy of imminent destruction unless they repented of their sins. Jonah preferred them dead. Of course we know the story of Jonah being swallowed by a fish then vomited on dry land. He then decided that doing what God asked was best.
     On this second appeal by God, Jonah went to Nineveh, a large city that took three days to see everything. He began to evangelize, brings God's words to the people. However, things did not go as he expected. People listened. The prospect of being dead in 40 days cut to their heart. Even the king sat up and took notice. He declared a fast and asked that everyone repent or be destroyed.
     Over the next 40 days an entire nation listened and turned to God. As a result, Nineveh became a Godly nation.

When God saw what they did and how they turned from their evil ways, he had compassion and did not bring upon them the destruction he had threatened. Jonah 3:10

What could happen if you shared God's word over the next 40 days?
Could a nation be saved?
Could a political leader follow God's direction?
Jonah was not very cooperative. He didn't exactly want to see Nineveh repent. Even after the second time, Jonah's heart was not completely into it. In Jonah 4, it says Jonah got mad at God for relenting on his destruction of Nineveh.

If God used an uncooperative, stubborn, prejudiced prophet to convert a nation, imagine what He can do with you...

You're a nice person. You have nice friends. You love them. God can use niceness far better than prejudice, but even if He has to use a prejudiced person, He can. His word is that powerful.

In 40 days, God's word convicted people of their sins.
In 40 days, God's word softened their hearts.
In 40 days, God's word turned them from a barbarian nation of ruthless killers to a repentant people, sorry for their sins.

In 40 days, what can God's word do in the lives of those you love?

We tend to think that God's word ranks in power with the words of Thomas Jefferson or Susan B. Anthony or Martin Luther King Jr. While their words brought freedom and change to a people, nation and country, those changes only occurred on earth. Jefferson's words freed America. Susan B. Anthony helped to give women's rights. Martin Luther King Jr. led the movement for Civil Rights. All of them important and powerful, but limited.

God's word brings freedom for eternity, healing the relationship between God and man.

Are you ready to see God's word bring freedom to those around you? This is a great time to renew your appreciation for God's word and its power to change lives. Tell others what you know and what you've learned about God.

Who knows, maybe the whole city will be turned upside down...

TODAY'S 40 DAY CHALLENGES

Read: John 1:1-18

Pray: Dear God, your Word is powerful and living and active. I must listen to it especially in the area of...

Do: What has God's word done for you? What would you like it to do?

Day 33

40 Days with Jesus' Temptation

Deserts

At once the Spirit sent him out into the desert, and he was in the desert forty days, being tempted by Satan. He was with the wild animals, and angels attended him. Mark 1:12-13

    If you've ever been on a cruise, you know it's days and days of activities, recreation, fun and eating. Buffets around every corner. Friendly servers there to meet your every need. Cool ocean breeze, refreshing drinks and your own personal cabin. Sound nice?
    Now, everything that a luxurious cruise is—Jesus' 40 days in the wilderness was not.
    Days and days of isolation and loneliness.
    Harsh, unrelenting elements.
    Nothing to eat.
    No one to greet you but wild animals.
    Satan.
    It sounds a lot like hell and maybe it was supposed to be.
    This was quite an introduction to Jesus' three year ministry. Maybe a prerequisite. Imagine if your job's training required you to go 40 days without food or water in the harshest of elements, facing off with your competition who was well fed and in great shape.
    Jesus was in the weakest position possible before He squared off with Satan...
    Physically—no food or snacks.
    Relationally—no friends or family.
    Emotionally—no human encouragement.
    Yet, despite Jesus' deficiency in the other areas, He wasn't lacking in the most important—spiritually.

You can't say Jesus defeated Satan because He had been working out and eating a high protein diet. You can't say Jesus defeated Satan because He had twelve advisors, three lawyers and a couple bouncers standing nearby. You can't say Jesus defeated Satan because He was on his home turf.

Jesus showed us that even if everything looks desolate around us, we still have our spirit. We can't control the outside elements all the time, but we can control the inside element. While the visible signs of comfort and relaxation go away, the invisible is still in place ministering to us.

Besides the crucifixion, this was the worst possible physical predicament Jesus would face on Earth. It happened at the beginning of His ministry to show Satan that any efforts in bringing Jesus down for the next three years would be futile. If Jesus beat Satan all alone in the desert, He could beat him any other time in the future.

What you are currently going through may be the worst possible desert you've ever been through? You may feel alone, restless, starving for comfort, begging for refreshment. There are no friendly faces around you. You feel under attack. If so, there are two things to remember:

One, you are not alone. God knows your situation and He has sent angels to minister to you. Satan can hurl temptations and insults at you, but that's about it. He's all talk. It's up to you whether you'll listen to him or to the ministering sounds of God and His army all around you.

Second, winning this battle will help you win future battles. Survive Satan's attack now and you'll be stronger for the next. His attacks will seem less severe since you are better equipped and more spiritually in-shape to take the blows. Right now you can create a milestone to refer to in the future.

"Satan, you tried to defeat me before, but I have God and the heavenly host on my side. There was nothing you could do to me then and there is nothing you can do to me now."

But if you fail this time, it will be harder the second time to succeed.

Renew your commitment to win this next victory in the desert, prepare yourself spiritually and then you will cruise through other dry spots in your life more easily.

TODAY'S 40 DAY CHALLENGES

Read: 1 Corinthians 10:13, 2 Corinthians 11:16-33, 12:9-10

Pray: Dear God, help me to be strong during this time in the desert. I am weak in the area of...

Do: Walk for a mile today. While you "get strong" physically, pray about the area you are weak in.

Day 34

40 Days with Jesus' Temptation

Bread

Then Jesus was led by the Spirit into the desert to be tempted by the devil. After fasting forty days and forty nights, he was hungry. The tempter came to him and said, "If you are the Son of God, tell these stones to become bread." Jesus answered, "It is written: 'Man does not live on bread alone, but on every word that comes from the mouth of God.'" Matthew 4:1-4

    Almost every culture has bread. Bread is the mainstay of every diet. From Italian bread, to Greek pita, to Middle Eastern flatbread, to sourdough in San Francisco, if there's food in a culture, there is bread.
    Just watch any movie. When the character returns from the grocery store, there's a tall loaf of Italian bread sticking out of the top of the grocery bag. Trust me.
    Bread is filling. Bread provides nutrients our bodies need. Bread complements any dinner. Bread is good. There is nothing evil about bread.
    I can't imagine being on the Wilderness Diet for 40 days, totally Atkins-free, and all of a sudden Satan tempts me with bread. The smell. The warm texture. Maybe a little soft, creamy butter to drizzle on top.
    Satan struck a low blow by attacking Jesus at His physical need. It was the first temptation. Why? Satan believed Jesus was weakest in this flesh—the flesh He had so little experience inside of. The flesh caused the downfall of Adam with tasty fruit. Why not Jesus and bread? All it took was one mistake and Jesus would be disqualified from His Messiah status.

But the bread temptation was a strange one. What's wrong with offering bread to a starving person in the desert? Seems like the humane thing to do.

Satan's motivation was the problem. Satan suggested that Jesus break a spiritual fast to satisfy His physical need. Satan wanted Jesus to make the *physical* a priority, not the *spiritual*. Jesus rebuked him and referenced the Old Testament:

Be careful to follow every command I am giving you today, so that you may live and increase and may enter and possess the land that the LORD promised on oath to your forefathers. Remember how the LORD your God led you all the way in the desert these forty years, to humble you and to test you in order to know what was in your heart, whether or not you would keep his commands. He humbled you, causing you to hunger and then feeding you with manna, which neither you nor your fathers had known, to teach you that man does not live on bread alone but on every word that comes from the mouth of the LORD. Deuteronomy 8:1-3

The food we need…the really good food…the satisfying food…the food that fills us up…the food that provides us with the nutrients we really need…the food that complements everything…is the Word of God.

Jesus re-emphasized this later by saying He was the bread of life (John 6) and the word of God (John 1).

We are tempted every moment with two options—you may sense them consciously or they may sneak up on you unconsciously. Those two temptations are to feed our flesh or to feed our spirit. Will I do what the world wants me to do or will I do what God wants me to do?

Many of us need to go on a diet—a spiritual diet. However, this diet requires you to eat more of God's food—word by word, page by page, chapter by chapter. It runs counter to the every physical diet. Then again, the flesh and

the spirit are always total opposites, so that comes as no surprise.
  Renew your commitment to this spiritual diet and dine on the Word of God. Shovel it in. There's plenty more where that came from.

TODAY'S 40 DAY CHALLENGES

Read: John 6:25-59

Pray: Dear God, I need to consume more of your word. I have ignored it for too long, now I need to…

Do: Make a commitment to read at least a chapter a day of the Bible. After you read it, think about it. Apply it. Like a fine meal, you wouldn't hurry through it, would you?

Day 35

40 Days with Jesus' Temptation

View

Then the devil took him to the holy city and had him stand on the highest point of the temple. "If you are the Son of God," he said, "throw yourself down. For it is written:
" 'He will command his angels concerning you,
 and they will lift you up in their hands,
so that you will not strike your foot against a stone.'"
Jesus answered him, "It is also written: 'Do not put the Lord your God to the test.'"   Matthew 4:5-7

The second temptation has everything to do with your point of view.

Satan gave Jesus a reprieve from the boring sights of the wilderness and gave Him a wonderful view of the Holy City, Jerusalem, from on top of the temple. Then Satan pulled a Fear Factor and challenged Him to jump. Satan assured Jesus that He would be fine and quoted Scripture to prove it.

For he will command his angels concerning you to guard you in all your ways; they will lift you up in their hands, so that you will not strike your foot against a stone.   Psalm 91:11-12

Again, what's wrong here? Satan spoke truth. God would not let anything happen to the Messiah. Satan appeared to have more faith in angels than Jesus did. Satan wished no physical harm to happen to Jesus.

Satan's downfall was a power struggle. From his point of view, he was in charge. Satan wanted to tell Jesus what to do. Jesus countered him with Scripture. It came from the Old Testament and was spoken by Moses:

Do not test the LORD your God as you did at Massah. Be sure to keep the commands of the LORD your God and the stipulations and decrees he has given you. Do what is right and good in the LORD's sight, so that it may go well with you and you may go in and take over the good land that the LORD promised on oath to your forefathers, thrusting out all your enemies before you, as the LORD said.   Deuteronomy 6:16-19

Jesus told Satan, "Look, you don't tell me what to do. I tell you what to do."

In life, you are either a leader or a follower. Some of us are leaders at our places of work or in our areas of influence. Some of us are followers. When it comes to God, we are all followers. We may have leadership responsibilities under God, but we still follow His lead.

This is a hat trick of temptation. First, Satan tried to trick Jesus into jumping. Second, Satan tried to tempt God by commanding His angels. Third, Satan tried to tempt the angels into a rescue mission. He wanted everyone to answer to Him. "Do this…" "Go there.." "Change that…" Bossy, huh?

From our point of view, we need to know who is in charge. It's not us. We can certainly put our requests in, but our orders are clear—follow the commandments, the Bible and God's Holy Spirit. God may honor our requests or he may not. His decisions are final. He's the boss.

For us, our point of view is also a little off. We think we are standing pretty high up on the social, economic or popularity platform, but the truth is, God is always higher. Don't be tempted to idolize yourself.

Renew the view of your life and get down off your temple.

TODAY'S 40 DAY CHALLENGES

Read: Genesis 11:1-9

Pray: Dear God, I am sorry that I've tried to tell you what to do. I need to listen to what you want me to do, especially when it comes to...

Do: Ask someone if there is something you can do for them today (then do it). Think about how this applies to your relationship with God. Do you ask him then do it?

Day 36

40 Days with Jesus' Temptation

Promotion

Again, the devil took him to a very high mountain and showed him all the kingdoms of the world and their splendor. "All this I will give you," he said, "if you will bow down and worship me." Jesus said to him, "Away from me, Satan! For it is written: 'Worship the Lord your God, and serve him only.'" Then the devil left him, and angels came and attended him. Matthew 4:8-11

King of the Hill is a pretty fun game. You find a hill and everyone runs up it, then you start throwing people off the hill. Then one emerges as the king because he's stronger. But continuous attacks from all sides weaken the king and eventually someone gets the best of him and throws him down. This keeps going until everyone gets worn out, quits, goes home or someone hears their mommy calling.

The final temptation during Jesus' 40 days in the desert revolved around promotion. It was a spiritual game of King of the Hill.

Satan, in desperation, took Jesus to an even higher point of view than the temple. This one looked over the whole earth! Satan told Jesus, "I'll give it all to you."

Think about the ramifications of that...Jesus could be the King of the Earth. He could fix all the political problems, health problems, wealth problems, society problems. Our time on earth could be paradise if Jesus took the offer. But it came with a price. Worship Satan.

Jesus denied Satan and again quoted Scripture:

Fear the LORD your God, serve him only and take your oaths in his name. Do not follow other gods, the gods of the peoples around you; for the LORD your God, who is among you, is a jealous God and his anger will burn against you, and he will destroy you from the face of the land. Deuteronomy 6:13-15

    Was Jesus saying He didn't care about the state of the world? Did He turn down the job because He didn't love us? Not at all. His later words and actions show us He does care and He does love us. But something else was at stake here.
    Promotion. Satan claimed ownership of the earth. He was willing to give Jesus the position of Vice President of Earthly Affairs. Sounds pretty good, huh? For you and I, yes, that would be a big step up for us. For Jesus, no, it's a huge step down. He is already the Founder, Chairman, CEO and CFO of the Universe. Satan's offer was a demotion.
    Satan offered to take his hands off the day-to-day affairs of the earth if Jesus would take over the job...and answer to him. Therein lies the catch.
    Jesus loved us too much to take the demotion. He acknowledged through this situation that the day-to-day affairs and struggles we face on earth are nothing compared to the position that Jesus rules unopposed...as heavenly King. The worldly is tough and difficult, but it's not what life is all about. The heavenly is where true power resides and what really matters.
    Unable to penetrate Jesus' holiness, Satan departed to reorganize his attack, including, now, such pawns as Judas, the religious leaders and Romans. They were a much more compliant group to work with. Satan was wasting his time with Jesus.
    The struggle must have been wearing on Jesus' earthly body because the angels stepped into the ring after the final bell to attend to Him. 40 days of fasting without food or water, all alone and in the flesh, Jesus needed some reassurance.
    Our struggle with Satan gets pretty tiring too. We must remember three things:
    One, God is in control. He is the King of the Hill.

Two, God's word can throw Satan down off his pedestal.

Three, we have help—angels are waiting to minister to us.

Over these 40 Days, Satan will try to throw you down too. Stand firm and resist. There's a promotion in it for you too.

TODAY'S 40 DAY CHALLENGES

Read: Revelation 19

Pray: Dear God, you are in control. You are all authority and power. I am only a...

Do: Go somewhere with a view (an upper story, a building, a mountain, in an airplane). Look down and around. It's all God's.

Day 37

40 Days with Jesus' Resurrection

Seeing

In my former book, Theophilus, I wrote about all that Jesus began to do and to teach until the day he was taken up to heaven, after giving instructions through the Holy Spirit to the apostles he had chosen. After his suffering, he showed himself to these men and gave many convincing proofs that he was alive. He appeared to them over a period of forty days and spoke about the kingdom of God. Acts 1:1-3

  After Jesus' trial, execution and burial, His disciples were in a state of confusion and panic. If the leader was dead, they wondered, what would happen to the followers? Word spread quickly on that Friday afternoon throughout Jerusalem and rippled into the surrounding areas of Judea and Samaria.
  "Remember that guy who came through town and healed all those people?"
  "Yeah."
  "He's dead."
  "What! I liked him."
  For three years, Jesus' popularity had spread and now the news was desperate. This man who said He was the Son of God had been killed by Roman soldiers. Bad news travels fast.
  That all changed Sunday morning. Jesus stepped out of the tomb with a brand new, shiny body. He was alive. Everything He said was true. Everything He promised came to life. Now good news had to travel faster.
  During the 40 days, Jesus wanted to give everyone convincing proof that He was alive. What convincing proof did the people need?

The most convincing proof of all—they saw Him. Paul talks about this:

> For what I received I passed on to you as of first importance: that Christ died for our sins according to the Scriptures, that he was buried, that he was raised on the third day according to the Scriptures, and that he appeared to Peter, and then to the Twelve. After that, he appeared to more than five hundred of the brothers at the same time, most of whom are still living, though some have fallen asleep. Then he appeared to James, then to all the apostles, and last of all he appeared to me also, as to one abnormally born. 1 Corinthians 15:3-8

For 40 days Jesus went on a public relations tour to heal the premature rumors of his demise. He wanted to show them that death had not had its victory. In fact, death lost terribly in the final seconds. It was the greatest comeback of all time. And people saw it with their own eyes. Paul even challenged the readers of this letter—some of those that saw Jesus were still alive if anyone wanted to go talk to them.

Today, we cannot receive the same convincing proof that 500 others had 2,000 years ago. We cannot have face-to-face, eye-to-eye contact with Jesus or one who saw Jesus. Out of the millions that believe in Christ's resurrection up to this day, only 500 or so had real proof. The rest of us have a different kind of proof.

The Bible is an accurate document that has stood up to intense scrutiny. Extra historical sources from that period verify the time, place and people mentioned in the Bible.

The truth proclaimed in the Bible still makes sense logically, socially, philosophically.

The incredible transformation of these once cowardly apostles into bold, evangelistic men says something amazing happened during those 40 days.

And Jesus appears to many today, in different ways. Changed lives testify to the ability of a still-living God working in the hearts of man. He still heals. He still feeds. He still gives life.

If you don't believe, ask someone what they have seen. If you do believe, tell someone what you have seen.

TODAY'S 40 DAY CHALLENGES

Read: **John 20**

Pray: **Dear God, you are alive. I know this because I've seen it with my own eyes…**

Do: **Write down three proofs that Jesus Christ is alive and working in your life.**

Day 38

40 Days with Jesus' Resurrection

Kingdom

In my former book, Theophilus, I wrote about all that Jesus began to do and to teach until the day he was taken up to heaven, after giving instructions through the Holy Spirit to the apostles he had chosen. After his suffering, he showed himself to these men and gave many convincing proofs that he was alive. He appeared to them over a period of forty days and spoke about the kingdom of God. Acts 1:1-3

For those 40 days while Jesus dispelled the rumors that He was dead, Jesus confirmed a message to everyone He encountered.
The Kingdom of God is at hand!
It was an issue that every Jew living in the Roman-occupied Promised Land wanted to discuss. As Jesus' 40 days of resurrection wrapped up and before he ascended into heaven, the apostles got together and asked:

"Lord, are you at this time going to restore the kingdom to Israel?" Acts 1:6

The kingdom of Israel? Whoops. Wrong kingdom. Jesus had been talking about another Kingdom. The bigger Kingdom. The universal Kingdom. The eternal Kingdom. The Kingdom that Jesus ruled over.
That's the problem with humans, we think too small. Our limited vision sees only our little kingdom, the here and now and what's across the street. We think the world is our town, our neighborhood, our house. God has a much bigger perspective, seeing beyond horizons in all directions.

The Kingdom of God encompasses all of time. God is an eternal God so His kingdom lasts through eternity.

The Kingdom of God extends throughout the known universe. It begins as close as your heart and extends to the farthest star billions of miles away.

The Kingdom of God rules the unseen universe. Angelic hosts patrol the invisible (to us), obeying the orders of the King on His throne.

The Kingdom of God contains all truth. Nothing false or deceiving is reported. No scandal is covered up or hidden.

The Kingdom of God is the source of all knowledge. Everything that has happened is known, as well as everything that will happen.

The Kingdom of God is ruled with love. The heart of the Kingdom reflects the heart of the King and His Son.

Sounds like a wonderful place. Who wouldn't want to be a part of that?

People come from all over the world to visit the Magic Kingdom in Walt Disney World, saving up money for years, taking time off from work, gathering their friends and family and spending beyond their resources. Why? For a week of recreation, hospitality and family bonding that they have dreamed about for years!

Many of us that live near the Magic Kingdom in Orlando have a different point of view. We have a seen-that, been-there, done-that attitude. We believe the Magic Kingdom will always be there when we want it to be there. Thirty minutes to drive, park the car, buy a ticket. We're in. But in the meantime, we'll just go on with our lives and maybe some weekend we'll stop by. The closer we live to the Magic Kingdom, the easier it is to take for granted.

Some day, the Magic Kingdom won't be there for us. Not because it's going anywhere, but because we are.

Have we somehow missed the wonder and beauty and power of the Kingdom of God? Do we find ourselves just outside its borders believing someday we'll visit, but knowing it'll always be there, so why bother now? Someday we'll buy our ticket. Someday we'll turn our minds to the Kingdom. The Kingdom of God is only accessible as long as our hearts continue to beat. After that and without our Eternal Pass, the Kingdom closes its gates to us. The time to visit this incredible Kingdom is only seconds away. Why would you want to reserve your place at the most incredible place in the universe?

TODAY'S 40 DAY CHALLENGES

Read: Luke 13:18-30

Pray: Dear God, I have taken your Kingdom for granted. I've thought of being a part of it, but put it off another day. Today, I want to commit...

Do: If you are a believer, renew your commitment to the Kingdom of God. If you not, tell God you want to join today.

Day 39

40 Days with Jesus' Resurrection

Resurrection

But if it is preached that Christ has been raised from the dead, how can some of you say that there is no resurrection of the dead? If there is no resurrection of the dead, then not even Christ has been raised. And if Christ has not been raised, our preaching is useless and so is your faith. More than that, we are then found to be false witnesses about God, for we have testified about God that he raised Christ from the dead. But he did not raise him if in fact the dead are not raised. For if the dead are not raised, then Christ has not been raised either. And if Christ has not been raised, your faith is futile; you are still in your sins. Then those also who have fallen asleep in Christ are lost. If only for this life we have hope in Christ, we are to be pitied more than all men. 1 Corinthians 15:12-19

Those 40 days that Jesus walked the earth in His resurrected body meant everything! Jesus did not resurrect in private or hide in the shadows. He made sure many saw the truth. Paul discussed in length the value of that resurrection message.

If there is no resurrection of the dead, then Jesus did not come back to life and He's still dead in the tomb. If He's still dead in the tomb, then He was just a man and he lied. We were fooled.

If there is no resurrection of the dead, then those that believed and testified about this Good News are also liars.

If there is no resurrection of the dead, then every sermon ever preached, every book ever written, every word of the Bible is useless. All of it rested on the promises of God to give us forgiveness and life through an eternal sacrifice. If that sacrifice lies dead, then Jesus had no more power over death than a common sheep and could not keep His promise to save us. We are unforgiven.

If there is no resurrection of the dead, then all those who ever died will remain dead, rotting in their graves, turning to dust and blowing away. All hope is lost.

If there is no resurrection of the dead, then our trust in God and our faith in Jesus Christ are futile. Our faith is useless.

If there is no resurrection of the dead, then believers should be pitied for being so stupid.

On the other hand...

But Christ has indeed been raised from the dead, the firstfruits of those who have fallen asleep. For since death came through a man, the resurrection of the dead comes also through a man. For as in Adam all die, so in Christ all will be made alive. But each in his own turn: Christ, the firstfruits; then, when he comes, those who belong to him. Then the end will come, when he hands over the kingdom to God the Father after he has destroyed all dominion, authority and power. For he must reign until he has put all his enemies under his feet. The last enemy to be destroyed is death. For he "has put everything under his feet." Now when it says that "everything" has been put under him, it is clear that this does not include God himself, who put everything under Christ. When he has done this, then the Son himself will be made subject to him who put everything under him, so that God may be all in all. 1 Corinthians 15:20-28

Since Jesus was resurrected, then He is the first example of what others will experience.

Since Jesus was resurrected, then all will be made alive.

Since Jesus was resurrected, then we all belong to Him.

Since Jesus was resurrected, then He will reign forever and subdue the enemy.

Since Jesus was resurrected, then He must be worshipped and followed.

Whether you believe Jesus was resurrected or not makes all the difference to the ultimate renewal you will experience when you too are resurrected.

TODAY'S 40 DAY CHALLENGES

Read: **Acts 2:14-41**

Pray: **Dear God, your resurrection makes all the difference. I believe you were resurrected, which means, for me...**

Do: **Calculate the cost of believing. Then calculate the cost of not believing. Which is better?**

Day 40

40 Days with Jesus' Resurrection

Go

After he said this, he was taken up before their very eyes, and a cloud hid him from their sight. Acts 1:9

After 40 days of proving His resurrection, Jesus took his followers to the Mount of Olives overlooking Jerusalem. From there they had a view of the Holy City and much of the surrounding area. They could see the site of the Triumphal Entry where many declared Him the Messiah. They could point out some of the areas where Jesus healed the sick and rebuked stubborn religious leaders. From this vantage point, they could see the place of His crucifixion and where the disciples hid, hopeless and scared.

All of the good times and all of the bad times.

But before Jesus departed, He wanted to leave them with these words:

..."All authority in heaven and on earth has been given to me. Therefore go and make disciples of all nations, baptizing them in the name of the Father and of the Son and of the Holy Spirit, and teaching them to obey everything I have commanded you. And surely I am with you always, to the very end of the age."
Matthew 28:18-20

Jesus wanted to make sure that they clearly understand their orders. No longer were they to hide in rooms, but to get out and proclaim what they had seen and what they knew. And what factor would motivate the disciples to do this? Because they wanted to? Sure. Because it was a good idea? Yes. Because it'll do a lot of good? You bet.

What's the real reason they needed to do what Jesus asked? Because Jesus is the boss. He encompassed all authority in heaven and on earth. And the boss had something for them to do. Were they going to say *no* to the boss?

It's His desire today that we get out and get busy. Like Jesus' disciples, we too have a renewed purpose and direction. Jesus makes those orders very clear. He gives us the WHAT, the WHERE and the WHEN to carry out His tasks.

Here is WHAT God wants you to do:
- GO – Get out of your comfort zone, unlock your door, visit a local homeless shelter, go on a mission, start a Bible study.
- MAKE DISCIPLES – Find others and make sure they become students of God's word. Help them.
- BAPTIZING – See them make public and total life commitments to God.
- TEACHING – Answer their questions, give them guidance, and reveal truth to others.
- OBEY – Follow all of the commands God has given us.

That's a lot to do and it will take the rest of our lives to see it done. So, WHERE are you supposed to carry out those orders:
- EVERYWHERE – "in all the nations" means the nation you live in all the way to some distant country.

That's a lot of places.

So WHEN should you be carrying out all those orders?
- ALWAYS – God asks us to carry out this final commission as long as He is with us and we are here on earth. We cannot do it alone. So, if He's with us always, meaning this moment until the end of the age, then we need to get to work now.

For 40 Days, it has all led up to this. We've studied and tested what God wants for our lives—His good, pleasing and perfect will. Our commitments, our perspectives our insights and our heart have all been transformed.

We've been renewed.

Now we need to bring renewal to the world around us—taking God's powerful transforming message to a world looking for a fresh start. It does not all stop with us. It begins with us.

What's stopping us?

TODAY'S 40 DAY CHALLENGES

Read: Revelation 22

Pray: God, I see clearly the final picture of renewal that you have for this world. A new heaven and a new earth. I know after these 40 Days that you want me to help bring that renewal by...

Do: What can the all-new, renewed-you do today? You can you help renew by telling them about God's renewal for their lives?

CONGRATULATIONS

You've made it.

40 Days has gone by. Now you know what it was like to sit through 40 days of rain, 40 days on a mountaintop, 40 days of taunting by a giant, 40 days sitting in a desert without food...

Well sort of. Hopefully it wasn't that hard.

It's time for a moment of reflection as you look over the renewal process.

What did you feel you renewed over the past 40 Days?

What do you feel you need to concentrate on?

Which devotion impacted you the most?

Which challenge challenged you the most?

THOUGHTS / PRAYERS / NEXT STEPS

ABOUT THE AUTHOR

Troy Schmidt began writing animation in Los Angeles in 1985 (*Dennis the Menace, Heathcliff, Flintstone Kids*). In 1992, he moved to Orlando to write for *The Mickey Mouse Club*, working on staff for three seasons. He adapted a Max Lucado children's book, *Hermie The Common Caterpillar*, into a video, then created and wrote all the future video installments and twenty Hermie books. Troy directed documentary footage in Israel for iLumina Gold, then returned in 2008 to host a documentary entitled "In His Shoes: The Life of Jesus" for GLO Bible software. In 2012, Troy was a producer and writer for the GSN game show "The American Bible Challenge" starring Jeff Foxworthy.

Troy is married to Barbie and has three grown boys, Riley, Brady and Carson. He is a campus pastor on staff at First Baptist Church Windermere, Florida.

WEBSITES

Personal writing page – **www.troyeschmidt.com**

Apologetic/Bible Q&A – **www.reasonhope.com**

Church dramas – **www.churchscriptsonline.com**

Testimonies and salvation – **www.iamsavedsite.com**

BOOKS

"40 Days: A Daily Devotion for Spiritual Renewal" (Amazon)

"Saved: Answers That Can Save Your Life" (Amazon)

"Release: Why God Wants You to Let Go" (Amazon)

"Praying Through Genesis" (Amazon)

"Living the Real Life:
12 Studies for Building Biblical Community" (Amazon)

"Laughing Matters" (Lillenas Publishing)